NETBALL TODAY

NETBALL TODAY

Phyl Edwards M.A.

Senior Lecturer, Department of Sport and Recreation Studies,
Liverpool Polytechnic

and

Sue Campbell M.Ed., Dip. Ed., Dip. P.E.

Regional Officer,
The Sports Council – East Midland Region

LEPUS BOOKS · LONDON

© Lepus Books 1981
An associate company of Henry Kimpton Ltd
7 Leighton Place, Leighton Road, London NW5 2QL

British Library Cataloguing in Publication Data

Edwards, Phyl
    Netball Today.
    1. Netball
    1. Title   2. Campbell, Sue
    796.32   GV887

ISBN 0 86019 049 8

Printed in Great Britain at the
University Press, Cambridge

Foreword

by Liz Nicholl, Director, All England Netball Association

Millions of schoolgirls and adults spend hours each week playing one of their favourite, traditional games—NETBALL. They can enjoy their game all the more as a result of the contribution from some of the many umpires and coaches currently holding awards given by the All England Netball Association.

Phyl Edwards and Sue Campbell are two very talented coaches with vast experience at every level of participation, and they have successfully moulded their thoughts together in this book to produce a comprehensive guide to the modern game of netball. Each and every aspect of the game has been closely analysed to give guidance to both coaches and players, and the importance of obtaining feedback and providing motivation are stressed. Additionally a number of tasks have been suggested as a way of familiarising participants with the body movements required to perfect the necessary techniques in the game.

The skills incorporated into attacking and defensive actions, and the two essential ingredients of cooperation and competition—which need to be finely blended—are also discussed. Other aspects of the game, such as Set Pieces and Tactics, are also scrutinized and advice is given on warm-up procedures and fitness training. This book, I am sure, will stimulate even the most experienced participant to think more about their game . . . NETBALL.

January 1981

Foreword

by Prof. Dr. H.T.A. Whiting, Vrije Universiteit, Amsterdam

The title, *Netball Today,* symbolises the state of 'becoming' so peculiar to any game; change and progress is inevitable. It reflects not only changes in the structure and rules of the game—which have given greater fluidity and appeal—but also changes in the approach to the game by both players and coaches. It is in this latter respect that Phyl Edwards and Sue Campbell have made their greatest contribution. They have done this by adopting a critical analysis of the playing units within the game, based both on first-hand extensive knowledge of netball at all levels and on those psychological principles of skill acquisition and training which they show to be so vital. In so doing they have produced a technically sound book that is also practically appealing.

What is offered, then, is not a 'cook-book' or set of rules to be followed, but a flexible framework that will enable the committed player or coach to apply such systems, as are offered, to the context in which they are working. For this reason alone it is likely to be a number of years before *Netball Today* becomes outdated. An active involvement, rather than a passive reception of information, by the reader is necessary if maximum success is to be achieved. It is necessary that time is taken to fully understand the principles adhered to in this book. This understanding will enable the reader to extend the range of examples and possibilities that a single book can present.

It is refreshing to read a practical book for coaches and players that can make an excellent synthesis between theory and practice. There is little doubt in my mind that this book will make a valuable contribution to a game which is fast-growing in popularity.

January 1981

Contents

Preface

Netball is an extremely fast game that takes place within a small area. It demands unwavering concentration and lightning decisions from its players and its rules make team work crucial. We believe that netball has something unique to offer players of all ages and ability, and consider it a worthy candidate for inclusion in any programme for girls or women.

It is basically a simple game which provides an enjoyable challenge for novices and international players alike and, as with all modern competitive games, there are many factors that need to be considered if the best results are to be achieved. Recent scientific developments have brought a new dimension into coaching and teaching and this is reflected in our approach to the game. We have attempted to apply our 'laboratory knowledge' to practical situations.

There is no *one* specific formula for success and we have therefore provided the ingredients for the teacher/coach to use in her own way. Individual style is vital if netball is to avoid becoming stereotyped. We hope that every player, teacher or coach will find this book stimulating and as a consequence develop their game with skill and flair.

Phyl Edwards

Sue Campell

January 1981

Acknowledgements

The authors are most grateful for the photographic work produced by Eric Blackadder, who is a lecturer in the Physical Education Department at Loughborough; to the many players who have suffered so enthusiastically under their instruction; to Philip Woodcock for drawing the line work from their original material; and finally to the support of the All England Netball Association.

1
The Game: An Introduction

THE MODERN GAME

Netball can be an exciting and stimulating game for everyone, whatever age or ability. Even at an elementary level it is a fast, energetic game that requires the active involvement of *all* the players. As the skill level improves there is a need for discipline, control and planning so that individual flair may be harnessed and developed into cohesive team play.

At the highest level, players need to be thinking as well as moving at great speed. 'Thinking' in any game is as much a skill as ball handling and distribution; forming a fundamental part of all lessons or coaching sessions. Played at international level, netball can best be described as 'chess on the move'; each player continuously assessing the rapidly changing situations, working out various possibilities, and making quick decisions. In chess, however, the final decision may not be made for many hours, whilst in netball the whole process can take less than one second. Each player must therefore be trained, at the earliest stages of learning netball, to observe, assess and make their own decisions. It is not meant by this that there is a high level of complexity involved in the game. Rather it is the basic simplicity of netball which is one of its main attractions. What is meant is that, where applicable, players should be encouraged to question and contribute to training sessions in order that they may develop decision-making strategies alongside physical expertise.

ORIGINS OF NETBALL

Games similar to netball were played in ancient times by the Greeks and Romans. *Trugon* was a Roman game for three players in which the main emphasis was on precise and fast ball handling. Controlled footwork and skilful ball handling were also of crucial importance in *phaimida* (Greek) and *harpastum* (Roman). Another team game played by the Greeks was *episkyros* which required an ability to dodge and mark in confined spaces. The Aztecs and other South American cultures also played a game which in its basic concept could be compared to basketball and netball.*

Netball, as it is known today, is a direct descendant of American basketball. Dr James Naismith, a Canadian working as a YMCA secretary in Springfield, Massachusetts, USA, introduced basketball in 1891. Four years later a fellow American, Dr Toles, introduced the game to Britain. He visited Madame Osterberg's College of Physical Training in North London in 1895 and taught the young ladies indoor basketball. There were no printed rules, no lines, no circles and no boundaries. The goals were waste-paper baskets hung on the wall at each end of the hall. In America there were three sets of rules for basketball and many schools and colleges changed the rules as they thought fit, resulting in numerous variations of the original game.

In 1899, an American woman paid a visit to Madame Osberberg's College, now removed from Hampstead to Dartford, and taught the game as it was then being played by women in her country. Rings and a larger ball were introduced, the ground was divided into three courts and some of the American rules adopted.

DEVELOPMENT OF NETBALL

The emergence of netball at this time was a significant step forward for women's sport. The Victorian attitude to women was generally discrimina-tory and repressive. The female in society was seen as inferior. Fitness was considered unfeminine and there was a belief that to display physical abilities was degrading to the female sex. Set against this background it was difficult for a woman's game to be accepted, but netball developed quite rapidly, due largely to the members of the Ling Association which was founded in 1899 by past students of physical training colleges. In 1901 they set up a special sub-committee to publish an official set of rules for netball, adopting many changes from the latest American rules.

As netball was included in the curriculum of physical training colleges, the game rapidly spread through girls' schools, especially in the cities and towns where space was limited. As the pupils left school many of them wanted to continue to play the game, and subsequently became founder members of netball clubs throughout the country.

After the First World War, with the realisation that women had made a significant contribution to the war effort, the attitude towards women changed considerably. The subsequent growth of the suffragette movement also helped to enlighten people to the needs of women. Reverend Thomas Boslooper summed up the problems for the emerging sportswomen in the 1920s:

'... Women have three basic rights; the first is political and the second is professional. Now women are fighting for the most basic of their rights, the physical right, the right to play, to be fit, to compete in sports and we are hearing the same argument again...that is that they will lose their feminity.' (Boslooper, 1967, *The Nature of Women and Some Reflec-tions on Aspects of Competition*. Battle Creek Curriculum Development Project, Michigan.)

Despite these cultural conflicts a joint committee of the Ling Association and the London Home Counties Federation was set up in 1925. They were to consider the formation of a national association, and on the 12th February 1926 a meeting was held in London with more than 230 delegates from schools, colleges, outside clubs and adult organisations. The meeting resulted in the formation of the All England Womens Netball Association, followed by the foundation of county associations.

During the Second World War nearly all competitive sport in Britain was curtailed. In the German-occupied Channel Islands, due to the lack of entertainment, netball began to flourish. After the War (in 1945) the annual inter-county tournaments were resumed under the organisation of the newly-named All England Netball Association.

It then became obvious that if netball was to develop further it would have to look to other nations for opposition. The first home international matches took place in 1949 with a triangular fixture between England, Scotland and Wales, but it was not until 1956 that an overseas team (Australia) visited England, and an England team toured abroad in South Africa. These were significant events, reinforcing Rena Stratford's statement at the Annual General Meeting of the same year: 'I think we must think now in terms of an International Federation'.

The International Federation of Women's Basketball and Netball Associations became reality in 1960 at a conference held in Ceylon and shortly afterwards, in 1963, the First World Tournament was held at the Chelsea College of Physical Education, Eastbourne, Sussex. Eleven countries competed, but unfortunately there were few spectators and this was seen as an important public comment on the game. 'To get right publicity and the right status desired, the game must emerge from the school playground' (Harris, 1963, addressing a AENA Council meeting). By the end of the tournament Australia had emerged as the World Champions, New Zealand were second and England took third place. Subsequently, the world tournament has taken place every four years; 1967 in Perth, Australia; 1971 in Kingston, Jamaica; 1975 in Auckland, New Zealand; 1979 in Trinidad.

Netball itself, has gone through many changes and its coaching methods have been reviewed and revised. In fact during the last century the philosophies underlying *all* sport have altered dramatically. Present day attitudes are, however, no less varied than they have always been and it is therefore important that every teacher/coach establish their own fundamental coaching principles.

TEACHING METHODS

The method of teaching or coaching varies according to factors such as the age, intelligence, physical ability, personality, motivation and commitment of a group under tuition. Every individual acquires skill at a different level, and will progress at different rates; also it is worthwhile to remember that groups and individuals respond in different ways. Therefore, no attempt should be made to treat each member of a given group alike, or to treat each group as comparable. Some individuals experience the utmost difficulty in achieving the simplest skills, and for them tactics may be a 'closed book'. The job of the coach is to stimulate and encourage such players and help them achieve optimal improvement commensurate with their level of ability, while at the same time ensuring that, above all, they get enjoyment from their sessions.

At the same time, and possibly in the same group, some players may give evidence of great potential for the game. Here the coach can strike a balance by providing these players with sufficient challenge to prevent them losing interest in the game, whilst not neglecting the less able student. This is most likely to occur at school level, as club and representative sides are playing out of choice and are *often,* but not always, of a similar standard.

At an introductory level, players will be at their *most similar* and, here, group coaching is most applicable. Each member of the group can work on the same aspects of the same skill but, as they develop, the need for individual coaching will arise. This may mean coaching the specific skills relative to different positions, or highlighting individual errors within any skill. For example, in coaching 'distribution of the ball', one player may release the ball too late, another may have an incorrect preparatory action, while a third may release it with the wrong trajectory; thus illustrating that within one skill a coach may need to accent many different aspects.

This book will give an understanding of the skills and tactics of the game and provide a 'springboard' from which ideas and individual style can be developed. Coaches, too, are individuals and no attempt should be made to mould into another coach's pattern of working. Coaches can be imitators, as opposed to innovators and, while no one would suggest that to borrow ideas is wrong, indeed it is often essential, the ideas proposed here have worked for us simply because they have been developed along with our individual styles of coaching, as well as the ability of the groups with which we have worked. It is therefore suggested that each coach take the fundamental principles presented here, which do not change, and apply them in their own way to the group with which they are currently working. In this way the trap into which so many games have fallen, namely of becoming too stylised and predictable, should be avoided. There is always room for individual flair, both in players and coaches. Each coach has strengths and weaknesses and their job is to help team members make the best use of their strengths, and to minimise their weaknesses, while at the same time attempting to do likewise themselves.

2
Fundamentals of Coaching

This chapter discusses those aspects of coaching which can be considered relevant to any game. While no clear distinction is made between coaching and teaching, references are made to their fundamental differences. It is suggested that each lesson or coaching session should have three underlying objectives:

Purpose
Activity
Enjoyment

How these are achieved depends on the coaching methods used, and the following is a basic format which each coach can adapt to suit her own purpose.

METHOD OF PRESENTATION

There is no one way to coach or teach game skills, but how each session is planned should depend on the age and level of ability of the group. The style of presentation can also vary during the season, with one method being adopted early in the season, and another towards the end when the players will have attained a greater understanding of the game and a higher level of skill.

Basically, two methods of presentation are considered here:
1 Progressive parts.
2 Whole–part–whole.

Whichever one is adopted it is essential that each session starts with some form of warm-up which not only serves to prepare the body for the physical stresses of the game, but also 'sets the scene' and mentally prepares the players for what is to follow. Warm-up may involve simple running with changes of speed, or hopping, springing, bounding activities (see ch. 12, p. 96). These can also be developed into simple 'tag' or relay activities, or they could reflect the game to follow by the practising of 'set pieces' such as centre passes, feeding the circle, or defending shots (see ch. 13: *Set Pieces*).

Progressive parts

With younger children, or the less experienced player who has little knowledge of the full game, the progressive parts approach is probably the most beneficial and can best be described as a 'building block method'. For example, if a wall is knocked down its reconstruction follows a pattern of laying bricks adjacent to and on top of each other. By using this method in teaching, the skill to be taught is broken down into *realistic* parts. The reconstruction of a skill into its natural whole is done in successive stages, or progressions, by linking one skill part to the next. On whatever basis a skill is to be broken down prior to reconstruction, the following formula can be applied across the board.

Initially, the individual is allowed to work alone without the added distraction of another player. Then she is placed in a situation where she works in cooperation with one or more players, so that she now has factors other than herself and the ball to consider. Once a skill pattern has been established, she is placed under 'stress' by changing 'cooperation' to 'competition'. This will probably reduce her level of performance, but eventually she will learn to cope with such competitive pressures. The early introduction of competition is most important because games are competitive, and competing is an integral part of playing them. Competitive situations should therefore be increased in complexity and difficulty as the skill level increases.

The final section of the lesson, or session, taught in this way is the introduction of a game. This is the climax of the session and, while it may not be a full seven-a-side game, it should at least be competitive and rule-governed, with a scoring system. The skills which have been acquired should now be stressed and this may be achieved by the game being *conditioned*. This means imposing another 'rule' or 'condition' on the game. An example of this may be when a team's passing is being intercepted because it is too high and 'loopy'. The condition introduced here could be any pass above head height means a free pass to the opposition from where the ball was played. It is important that the relevance of the practices are emphasised to players because if they cannot see the point they may well develop a resistance to performing them.

Whole–part–whole

The presentation of skill as a whole, or in parts, depends on the complexity of the skill itself, and the ability of the players. Firstly, what constitutes a whole? Is it the whole game, the 'whole' throwing action, or the 'whole' foot rule? In their own way, each can be considered as a 'whole', but to the experienced player it might be the whole game, or a whole defence tactic. This 'whole' can be broken down into constituent parts and re-built. However, to beginners, such a 'whole' can be too complex to be absorbed, and therefore coaching is best restricted to a specific type of pass, or the foot-rule. These can then be analysed 'part-by-part' and built into a 'whole'.

Using the 'whole–part–whole' method of coaching, each session begins with a warm-up, following which the teams are put into a full game. While observing the game the coach selects aspects in which there is the greatest weakness (and is creating faults) which, with improvement, will improve the standard of play. Having selected this weakness, the coach stops play and works on the specific part concerned.

This is not to suggest that a coach who is dealing with a team throughout a season should *not* base decisions on what to coach by the team's least competitive performance, but what the coach should be wary of is setting out with preconceived ideas of what *she wants* to coach rather than what actually needs attention. It is of course essential to have forward planning and objectives set for the year's progress, but the speed of progress *must* be set by the group, and not by what is written in a scheme of work.

Depending on the level of ability of the group, the coach needs to approach the next step differently. With advanced players the skill or tactic concerned may be analysed both verbally and practically, but, with younger or less able groups, it may serve to break the skill down into component *parts* to be built together into a game-like *whole*. As with progressive parts, the sequence is the same with the players working in a simple unpressurised situation not unrelated to the real game. As skill develops the following sequence should be practised:

1 At the speed at which it will be done in the full game.
2 In the time allowed in the game.
3 With the type of opposition encountered in the game.
4 In the area of the court in which the skill will be used in the game.

A coach may feel that players do not need to analyse a skill, but rather perform it under pressure. An example of this may be by putting pressure on one player by having two or even three other players feed her balls to shoot for goal. This keeps her under greater pressure than in a normal game situation.

Immediately after skill or pressure training, the players should return to the whole game. A condition can then be placed on the game to emphasise the work just covered. If one skill session is not enough, it may be beneficial to leave the conditioned game, and once again work on the skill aspect. Whatever the case, it is suggested that the lesson or session be finished with a game, and, where possible, a normal and unconditioned one. The coach also needs to be prepared for a 'fall off' in the performance level of the players during this time. The reason for this is that though players may master the skill very adequately while working in individual and small group situations, once they are in the game they have so many other things to attend to that a drop in skill is to be expected. In the long term, improvement will be seen and therefore the coach should avoid feeling too despondent at these apparent 'drops' in skill, particularly as this dissatisfaction may well communicate itself to the players.

GUIDANCE

Verbal

The coach must use simple and concise instructions to ensure that, as far as possible, she and the group are 'talking the same language' (jargon may be readily understood by other coaches, but may mean nothing to players). Also, the coach who keeps up a constant barrage of instructions is very likely to make the group stop listening. The use of the voice is very important in coaching and, firstly, it must be audible. This will of course be influenced by the environment in which the coach is operating. Many high-roofed games halls are acoustically very bad and moving the group nearer when giving relatively long instructions can save the voice and ensure that everyone can hear. Secondly, the voice should be expressive to make it more pleasant to listen to. Thirdly if the voice reflects, for example, the speed, power or urgency of a movement, this will give so much more meaning to instructions.

Visual

Visual guidance in skill learning is vitally important. People, in the main, learn much more quickly by watching *and* listening, as opposed to just listening. When demonstrating a skill, a model or reference pattern should be used so that players can make a comparison with their own perform-ance. It is also important that this model or reference pattern be understandable because its use is to give the players an idea of what the 'end product' looks like.

The demonstration must also be modified to suit the ability level of the group. There is little point in showing a skill to beginners at the speed of an international player because they will not know what to look for (i.e. it bears no relationship to anything they are capable of doing, and hence will give them no reference pattern for comparison). However, seeing the expert in action *can* be used as a motivational technique. For instance, it is helpful to show what the finished product will look like, but only for inspiration and not immediate imitation.

As players become more advanced, so speed and complexity of demon-strations will increase. Players are now seeing with understanding, and the relevant aspects of the demonstrations are recognisable. It is emphasised here, however, that the coach must never assume that players are seeing what she is seeing. It is coach's job to point out those aspects that are important within the demonstration. It is also advisable to show a demonstration more than once because players will see very little on first observation.

Each time a demonstration is shown the coach can further reinforce the visual image by giving verbal comment. Another important factor is to keep demonstrations as free as possible from all unorthodox movement. If the coach is demonstrating, she must be aware of any idiosyncrasies in her style and try to eliminate them. If she finds she cannot do this, then they must be pointed out to the observers as something not to be copied. For instance, one difference many coaches forget is left-handedness and the left-handed coach must point out that her demonstration will be different because of this; particularly when dealing with young players.

The 'mirror-image' presentation is another pitfall and it is helpful if the coach places the group in a position relative to the demonstration so that they are seeing it as they will be expected to try and reproduce it.

The position of the coach in relation to the group is very important. The coach who allows a group to crowd around her when she is talking and demonstrating will not be seen by those standing at the back. Players need to spread out so that there is sufficient space for the demonstration to take place and for *all* players to be able to observe. The group's position should be where they will see the demonstration as it happens in the game. This way they get a more realistic concept of what they are being asked to do.

Manual

Manual guidance, i.e. the coach physically moving the player through a movement, should be used as infrequently as possible, and usually as a 'last resort' when all else has failed. For example, a limb moved through a movement by someone else will not provide the learner with the same sensation of movement if they move it themselves. This form of guidance may, however, be necessary on some occasions, but its application should be sparingly applied.

FEEDBACK/KNOWLEDGE OF RESULTS

Without feedback it is likely that little or no learning will take place. Some activities have their own 'built-in' feedback. For example, a goal is either scored, or it is not. The feedback the coach must provide is that which the player would have difficulty in discerning for herself. For example, the failed goal. In the heat of the moment a player may be more concerned with retrieving her missed shot, and not with why it failed. It is the coach's job to point out the reasons for failure. Feedback must be as concise and accurate as possible, and be given as near as possible to the occurrence of the event. If this failure occurs in a practice situation the coach may immediately stop the game to point out why the goal was missed, or the move broken down. The players can then repeat the action making the appropriate corrections based on her feedback. However, if it happens in a match, the feedback can come in the form of a debriefing at halftime, or at the end of the game.

Where possible, the use of visual feedback in the form of video-tape recording is most effective. Here, the players see their own performance and the coach can point out the relevant points which serve to improve future performances. In using this form of visual aid, the coach needs to be wary of showing a performance which is so destructive to an individual that they are completely demoralised. Generally though, most coaches who have this type of aid available find it to be an invaluable form of post-game feedback. For instance, aspects such as timing of the move, which can be difficult to understand when expressed verbally, become crystal clear when players see it for themselves.

MOTIVATION

Motivation is extremely important in the coaching of any game. As a defined term it has no fixed technical meaning, but it can be used to describe a conscious feeling or desire, or as a synonym for drive. Motivation has in fact been interpreted in broad general terms as *an arousal to action to achieve some goal,* and it is the coach's job to try and achieve this in her team. How this is done will of course vary with different individuals, each one responding in different ways. Some players respond positively to praise and encouragement, others require sympathy, while others may require 'straight from the shoulder' criticism. These types of motivation can also be applied to one player in different sets of circumstances.

The coach must know her team, and how to use various methods to bring out the best performance under whatever conditions prevail. Where praise is used as a motivation the coach should beware of its over-use. If everything a player does is praised, this 'blanket praise' can lose its value and result in the player no longer being influenced by it. The coach must also beware of over-motivation; of building up the pre-match tension to such an extent that rather than achieving the optimal level of arousal for efficient performance it merely pushes players to a state which may have adverse effects on their performance. Sometimes, in attempting to provide motivation for players, the coach may have to manipulate feedback in order to achieve the desired goal. An example of this might be when using a slightly larger target in a skill. In this case the less able player, or group, will be able to achieve some success and, through this success, may be motivated to continue and eventually (possibly) improve.

ENJOYMENT

Working on the principle that 'if it's fun it cannot be effective' is far from the truth. In fact players are more likely to learn if they are operating in an enjoyable situation. What must be remembered is that enjoyment will mean different things to different players. To the county player it may be the satisfaction of a hard physical work-out, or a complex tactical discussion. To someone in a recreative class it might be merely playing netball without too many coaching points, or the continuous stopping of play for every infringement of the rules. To a group of upper secondary girls, with little interest in the game, it might be 'It's a Knockout Netball', which is one way of disguising what is in reality a competitive skill circuit. To young children, netball might be a novel game based on ball familiarisation skills. Whatever the reasons, and though the above aspects are different, there are certain similar underlying principles of enjoyment. First there is a need to find the optimum amount of physical exertion suited to the group. Netball is played for the experience of the physical activity specific to the game, and players can get a great deal of enjoyment from leaving the court feeling that they have been physically hard-worked, but not utterly exhausted.

Variety is also essential to enjoyment and this can make the job of coaching very difficult. It is not a question of variety for variety's sake, often it is the same aspect of the skill or game which is breaking down. The coach will therefore need to devise a variety of ways of working on that one aspect, because to keep on repeating the same drill, or unit skill, for hours on end will undoubtedly lead to boredom and possible frustration if success is not being achieved. It is not suggested the coach's work be fragmented (e.g. leaving something which is breaking down and trying something else), but rather to work in a new guise on the same aspect.

Novelty is another aspect of enjoyment and the introduction of a new skill will enliven a practice. This type of practice can sometimes have limited value in a true skill sense, but its real value is in regaining the flagging attention of the group, or relieving pressure in a very hard session.

Striking an even balance in practice is essential if enjoyment is to be gained by the players. Too much of one type of work can lead to boredom and lack of concentration. The coaching sessions should be structured so that the physical and mental aspects are off-set by some light relief. An even balance is also needed when coaching skills, pressure training, conditioned games and full games. The group that merely plays a game without stopping to analyse what they are doing will probably feel as unsatisfied as the group who spends the whole session practising skills but never gets to apply them in a game.

RELEVANCE OF COACHING

Players do need to see the relevance of what they are doing and the importance of this obviously varies with the ability or age of a group. If the coach is building up parts of a skill, it is necessary to ensure that players are positioned into the overall pattern of the game. Players working on isolated aspects of the game can be totally unaware of when and how skills are applied in the competitive game. It is therefore important that some sort of link is made to ensure they understand, as far as possible, the relevance of what they are doing.

Finally, fun and laughter should be engendered into even the most arduous or important session; even if they are playing in the World Tournament the next week, or the final of their local league. There must of course be a great deal of hard work in the lead-up to such events, but even top players can only take so much pressure. The introduction of a little laughter serves to relieve some of this tension and refreshes players for further hard work, as well as increasing their overall enjoyment of the game.

3
Ball Familiarisation

A 'safe pair of hands' is essential to the skilful netball player, and the relationship between hand, eye and ball is an integral part of the game. Players need to be encouraged, from the outset, to play with the ball as often as possible, in a wide variety of situations. These situations need not be those of formal netball, but be such that they challenge the player to achieve optimal mastery of the ball. To this end the concept of ball familiarisation is proposed. Rather than considering netball skills as being exclusively specific, one needs to look at the intrinsic 'processes' which underlie a wide variety of skills. The development of skill in netball may be facilitated by the extent to which this intrinsic process has been developed (e.g. ball handling). By such an approach the development of flexibility in the specific skills of the game will perhaps result in flair and inventiveness returning to netball.

BALL FAMILIARISATION ACTIVITIES

The concept of general ball skills may be used as a warm-up for experienced players and, for beginners, as a form of introduction to ball skills. Each activity is open-ended in that there is no strictly correct answer. Nevertheless, players attention must be drawn to the links between various activities and the skills of netball.

Where possible, there should be one ball per player. This does not have to be an official netball, any large ball will do. In fact for young children the use of large, coloured balls, or volleyballs, are more suitable. The activities outlined in this chapter are designed to give experience of playing with a ball in (1) high, medium and low levels, (2) gaining possession and travelling with it, and (3) having it in continuous and discontinuous possession (e.g. volleying, trapping and bouncing).

Skill in any game involves physical and mental factors and therefore the players mental or intellectual capacity should be directed. Concentration or attention is essential if the player is to be alive to the ever-changing situations which occur within the game. This aspect can be highlighted in the ball familiarisation activities by drawing the player's attention to the relevant cues in each situation and encouraging the selection of appropriate strategies to achieve success.

In all these ball familiarisation activities, players should experience (1) working alone, (2) cooperating with others, and (3) competing against self and opponents. The latter is most important. Games are competitive and as soon as possible competition should be introduced. The suggestion here is not a 'cut throat' competition, but a simple regulated one that has some form of scoring systems which results in a measurable end product. Above all it must be stressed that purpose, activity and enjoyment underlie these activities because they are not 'free' play where players present any answer to a task, but structured activities directed by the coach to ensure that skills are performed to the best of players' abilities.

Some of the activities outlined below do not necessarily relate specifically to netball (e.g. travelling with the ball being bounced), but the coaching points of each specific activity do need to be emphasised so as to encourage as rich a skill repetoire as possible, and make each session challenging and interesting.

The following ball familiarisation tasks are set out in a developmental pattern, working from the easy to the more difficult, and from simple activities performed alone to the development of these activities to game-like situations involving both cooperation and competition. The first activity, *Ball High in the Air,* is described more fully than any of the others so as to give a greater understanding of how each aspect can be developed.

Ball high in the air

Task One

Travelling freely, the player sends the ball into the air and then prevents it from falling to the ground (e.g. heading or volleying the ball, or playing it off the knee, wrist, arm, etc). This can be done with any part of the body.

N.B. The ball must not be caught or thrown.

Coaching points

The player must follow the flight path of the ball. This may prove to be difficult because the use of unfamiliar body parts will result in difficulty in controlling the ball, which will undoubtedly produce highly erratic flight patterns.

Attention also needs to be given to the adjustment of the player's base so that they are able to achieve a quick change of direction. A possible link can be made with the type of base adopted in close man-to-man marking in netball; namely, a small base with the use of short, quick steps to allow for the sudden changes of direction so necessary in maintaining contact with an opponent (in this case it is not an opponent, but a ball moving erratically through the air).

Encourage the use of a variety of body parts; with young children this will be fun, with older players the difficulty of ball control will make the tracking of the ball (and the adjustment of base) vitally important.

Task Two

Follow as for task one, but develop the practice into volleying, as in volleyball.

Coaching points

Encourage players to relax their fingers on receiving the ball. This will prevent them from making their hands into a rigid surface off which the ball will rebound.

The player's attention on the ball is again important, but in this task players should have gained more control of the ball, thus making its flight path more predictable. How feet are used is also essential and small base, with quick steps (as mentioned in task one) should be used.

How arms are used is also important and they should be flexed on receiving the ball and extended as it is sent away. At this point, control will be further achieved by the introduction of various strengths of volleys so that the ball is sometimes sent high in the air, and at other times kept close to the hands.

Task Three
Working alone, the player faces a flat surfaced wall. The task is to volley the ball continuously against the wall.

N.B. This activity is not for beginners.

Coaching points
The volley must be controlled so that it does not rebound too far and returns directly back to the sender.

A mobile base is necessary so that the player can adjust quickly; this is particularly important in the forwards and backwards direction. This task is also beneficial for improving strength in the hands of the more mature player.

N.B. This is a good pressure and strength training task for the hands of more mature players.

Task Four
Working in twos, with one ball. The players stand facing each other. The distance between the two depends on their ability, but normally a distance of 10′ should be adequate. The aim is to keep a continuous volley with players keeping their own scores.

Coaching points
Players must be encouraged to keep their eye on the ball. Where predictable flight paths are concerned, the experienced player need only watch the 'high spots' (i.e. those aspects which are important). In this instance, it is *attention* that is being taught, rather than visual tracking.

A mobile base is necessary, particularly back to forwards, and the players must bend their knees to dig the ball off the floor.

Develop the above into a competitive situation. For example, count the number of volleys each pair achieves before skill breaks down. In every case, where players are asked to keep a score, the score of each player/ group must be checked.

Task Five
One ball between two players, who stand parallel to each other facing a flat

surfaced wall. The ball is volleyed from player to player in a 'V' formation (Fig. 1).

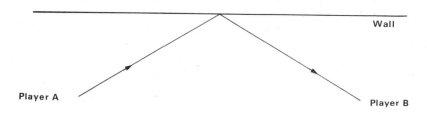

Fig. 1

The task should be cooperative, with players seeing how many volleys can be achieved before the skill breaks down.

Coaching points
The volley must be controlled so that the rebound is not too hard. The best way to achieve success in this skill is to get two players to volley the ball at a point on the wall equidistant between them, and above their head height.

It is important that the feet are used correctly so that the player can quickly adjust position according to the flight of the ball (see p. 13). Encourage players to keep their eye on the ball. The flight path of the ball in this task should be reasonably predictable, but it is important that the players attend to the *ball* at all times because the position of the other player can affect their skill only insofar as it will influence the flight of the ball.

Task Six
One ball between two players, who position themselves behind two parallel lines, facing each other. The distance between the lines depends on the skill of the players. The aim of this skill is to attempt to play the ball into a position where the opponent cannot reach, i.e. volley tennis. The players score a point every time the ball touches the ground in the opponent's 'court'. The number of points required to win, usually the first to reach 5 or 7 points, depends on the skill of the players. With advanced players, it is possible to make a direct link to netball with this skill because in some game situations the ball is passed in such a way that the receiver cannot gain clear possession, but merely contact the ball to either keep it in play or deflect it into space for another player to collect.

Task Seven
Divide players into threes (A, B, C) with one ball. The players form a triangle to start, although this formation can be more fluid as the skill develops. Player A feeds the ball high and well ahead of Player B, who does not attempt to catch the ball, but rather volleys it to Player number C. Player C must then try and 'read' the state of play and adjust her position so that she moves at the correct time to 'snatch' the ball out of the air.

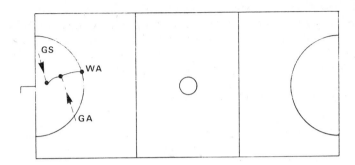

Fig. 2

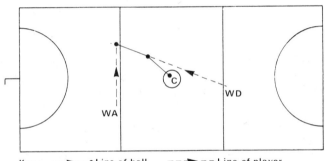

Fig. 3   Key: ——▶●Line of ball   — —▶ — —Line of player

This activity can be put into specific areas of the court, e.g. the circle. In this case the formation could be as follows:

Player A: Wing Attack (WA) who is attempting to feed the circle.
Player B: Goal Attack (GA) who is moving in to receive the pass.
Player C: Goal Shooter (GS) who has moved nearer the post than GA.

Wing Attack then feeds the ball in high and well ahead of Goal Attack who does not catch it but volleys it onto Goal Shooter who then snatches it out of the air and shoots for goal (Fig. 2).

A second example (see Fig. 3) could be:

Player A: Centre (C) who is passing the ball well ahead of
Player B: Wing Defence (WD) who is travelling towards her off-side, i.e. towards the attacking third,
Player C: Wing Attack who is positioned ready to move and receive a pass from WD.

As with the above skill, the second player does not catch the ball, but volleys it towards the attacking third where Wing Attack moves across to 'snatch' the ball out of the air.

N.B. *The foregoing are not considered tactics,* but are for use in an emergency only. Generally speaking, in these situations, it is better for a player to exert some control over the ball as opposed to merely swinging wildly at it in an attempt to keep it in play. However, this type of pressure training is only suitable for the advanced player.

Ball high in the air (palm uppermost)

Task One

One ball per player, who directs the ball into the air above head level and propels it upwards by inverting the hand, or hands, and tapping the ball from underneath.

Coaching points

The hands must be relaxed and attention focused on the ball. Both hands should be used, with particular emphasis given to the non-preferred hand. The base should be mobile to achieve the necessary changes of direction with the minimum delay.

Task Two

Two players (A and B) with a ball. Using the skill described in task one, Player A keeps the ball in the air. Player B tries to flick the ball out of her opponent's hand without making bodily contact.

Coaching points

Player A must always try to keep maximum distance between the ball and opponent.

Player B must watch the ball and adopt a base which will allow her to change direction (including springing into the air) with the minimum delay. The timing of Player B's move is also important and she should manipulate the situation by using feint dodges (see p. 68) so that she can best time her move to achieve success.

As Player B obtains possession of the ball, the roles of attacker and defender change and the players must be coached to react quickly to this tactical change.

A scoring system needs to be devised; one possibility being that the player to retain the ball for the longest period is the winner.

N.B. It is important to prevent this activity from becoming rough, and any bodily contact *must* be penalised.

Ball at medium level

Task One

One ball per player, who tries to juggle the ball in as many different ways as possible (e.g. spin the ball on the fingers, roll it around the hand).

Coaching points

The use of both hands must be encouraged (e.g. transfer from hand to hand), as well as moving the ball high, low, fast, slow, between the legs, and around the body. For example, moving the body by rolling on the floor and balancing the ball, and not losing contact with it.

Task Two
One ball between two players (A and B). Player A stands in a chalked circle of approximately 3′ diameter and, using one hand, keeps the ball away from Player B who remains outside the circle and attempts to flick the ball off her opponent's hand. With more experienced players it can be advantageous to do without the circle because the change of role from attack to defence is more realistic in that both players chase any loose ball and immediately set up a new game situation as soon as one player gains clean possession.

Ball in contact with ground

Task One
One ball per player, who dribbles (bounce) the ball whilst travelling. To develop this task further, match the rhythm of the bounce to the rhythm of the feet. Additionally, make up a sequence of bounces showing change of speed, direction and level. With two players (A and B), 'break the code' or sequence of having Player A work and show sequence, with Player B observing and then repeating Player A's sequence. Observation of an opponent is essential in all games and should be encouraged so that players begin to immediately analyse their opponents. For instance players are often unaware of left-handed players in their own teams, never mind their opponents, so observation on this point alone is important.

Also the natural rhythm of a player needs to be observed, i.e. how she moves (e.g. staccato burst of speed, or a continuous even movement). A defence which can make an attacker change her natural rhythm has already put the opponent under pressure, and this may therefore lead to a deterioration of their skill level.

Coaching points
Encourage (1) use of both hands, (2) change of direction, (3) speed and rhythm, and (4) flexibility of fingers and wrists. The position of the hand in relation to the ball (i.e. behind the ball directing it ahead) is also important. As already mentioned, it is necessary that players observe their opponent so that their analyses of them begins as soon as they know who they are.

Task Two
One ball per player, who moves freely, dribbles (bounces) the ball, but does not look directly at it. The task can be further developed by having all players dribbling, but avoiding collisions, in a confined space. The task can also be made more competitive by adding an opponent (i.e. one ball between two players—A and B). Player A, with the ball, must keep it away from Player B.

Coaching points
Player A (in the competitive situation) must screen the ball by putting her body between it and her opponent. Attention should be given to the timing of Player B's move to the ball so that when she gains possession she does not come into bodily contact. Timing is a very individual factor and, ultimately, it is only the player who can decide when to move. However, a verbal command of when to move can be given to the player, but beware that they do not become too dependent on this signal. After this initial assistance, the player must be encouraged to make her own decision, as she would indeed have to do in a game situation. Change the roles of the players as soon as possession changes hands.

Ball at floor level

Task One
One ball per player, who rolls the ball ahead, chases, bends down, gains possession, and snatches the ball into the body. This task may be developed by the player obeying the footwork rule (see p. 51 and the *Official Netball Rules,* A.E.N.A) as she gains possession of the ball. Further, again obeying the footwork rule, the player can pivot to change direction and roll the ball in the new direction.

Coaching points
Ensure that the player does not roll the ball too far ahead of herself. When attempting to gain possession the player must bend her knees to take herself down to the ball, snatching it as quickly as possible from the floor towards the centre of the body.

Task Two
One ball between the players, who are positioned as shown in Figure 4.

Fig. 4

The feeder (F) rolls the ball and the two players A and B chase the ball and attempt to be the first to gain possession.

This task can be developed as follows: Firstly, the player who fails to gain possession adopts the role of defender and from a 3' distance attempts to defend a pass from the successful player to the feeder. Secondly, add a move on the part of the Feeder to receive the return pass in the best possible position.

The above skill can be made more difficult by having the initial move made towards a line which bounds an 'off-side' area. The players not only have to attempt to achieve possession, but remain on-side and make a successful return pass.

Coaching points
Ensure that the player in possession of the ball obeys the foot-rule and always snatches the ball to a position away from her opponents, then returns it to her feeder as fast as possible. The player adopting the role of defender must always be 3' from the landing foot of the player with the ball.

SUMMARY

If the activities outlined above are followed, then players will gain experience in manipulating a ball in a number of ('game-like') situations. For example:

1 The use of a variety of levels: *high*—with volleying and tapping; *medium*—with juggling and bouncing; *low*—with rolling.

2 The use of a variety of body parts, with emphasis on the use of the hands. The volleying practice, for instance, will help strengthen wrists and fingers; so essential for strong accurate throwing.

3 Sending the ball towards a variety of targets, some of which have been static, e.g. a wall, or to a mobile target (i.e. another player).

4 The gaining or regaining of possession of the ball from a variety of angles and flight paths, and from different surfaces. In these situations the players have worked by themselves to control the speed and angle of the ball's flight, as well as, in more realistic situations, where they have had to deal with the variables of receiving a ball that has been set into motion by another player. In this instance, the coach or teacher should have been constantly drawing players' attention to the similarities between these activities and netball. For example:

a Eye on the ball, particularly when following an erratic flight path.

b The use of peripheral vision.

c The use of the hands and arms in receiving and sending a ball.

d The adoption of a base appropriate to the movement required, e.g. to spring or to change direction or to feint.

e The timing of the move, and the manipulation of play to create situations where timing is made easier.

f The immediate change of positional role to suit the changes in play, e.g. the sudden change from attack to defence when an attacking move breaks down.

g Above all, that games are competitive. As soon as the basic idea of a skill is acquired, it should be used 'competitively', e.g. 'How many times the ball can be volleyed without losing control' or 'Keep the ball away from an opponent'.

The skills of any activity are only the tools to be used to compete against another player or team. The skills are vitally important, but they are not an end in themselves. There is little point in being 'skill perfect' if these skills cannot be applied in the tactical situations of a game.

With older students the ideas in this chapter can be utilised as warm-ups or 'fun activities' to relieve the pressure or boredom of a continuous training regime—but *NOT* before competitive play.

4
Building a Game

Where ball familiarisation is used as an introduction to ball skills, each activity (e.g. Ball in contact with the ground—see ch. 3), can be used as a theme for a lesson.

Following a physical warm-up, such as running, hopping, bounding or skipping, the lesson should be developed using the following *formula:*

THE FORMULA

Exploration

The players explore and experiment individually with the idea being introduced. If possible, or where necessary, a ball each is an advantage, although this need *not* be a netball. The player attempts the set task (e.g. bouncing the ball while travelling), but has no external factors other than the ball itself to consider. In this way the number of variables to be considered is limited, therefore maximising the chances of success. The player also has sole control of the ball so that factors, such as the speed, level, and direction of the ball, are self-imposed. In this unpressurised situation, players will have the opportunity to internalise the basic elements of the skill being taught, and this discovery can be further aided by drawing attention to the important aspects of the skill. For example, when asked to bounce the ball, many may put their hand directly on top of the ball to direct it down (with the subsequent rebound being directly up) and when they try to move with the ball they will find they leave it behind. In this instance the players attention needs to be drawn to the fact that the hand must push the ball ahead so that it keeps up with them when they are running.

Competing alone

Games are competitive and skills are taught not as an end in themselves, but in order to play a game. As soon as possible some mild form of competition must be introduced, and the first level of competition should be the improvement of personal, best performance. This could be a simple form of contest, for example:

1 How many bounces can be achieved before control of the ball is lost.

2 How long the ball can be kept in the air before it touches the ground.

Always check the results. There is little point in competing if there is no outcome and, if the results are not checked, players may soon cease to keep their score and some of their interest may be lost.

Cooperation/competition with others

The blend of cooperation and competition is at the core of all games. As soon as players understand this concept it should be introduced into skill learning. For example, experimenting alone, players can be asked to share or cooperate with others in performing a skill. This will make their task one stage more difficult because now they not only have their influence on the ball, but also that of another person who may have a higher or lower level of skill than themselves. Even if players do not necessarily know the speed, level or direction of the ball, this task will help them start to observe and read such information. As with the individual play, cooperative play can be measured in terms of how many, or how long. *Again, always check results.*

The first simple form of competition against an opponent is a 1-v-1 situation. Many ball familiarisation tasks (see ch. 3) involve this type of activity, e.g. one player bouncing the ball with an opponent trying to take it away. Once this task has been introduced the concept of cooperating to compete can be used. To play team games successfully it is essential that players learn to cooperate with other players, blending their skills into the team unit. This can be done very simply at first by following on developmentally from the 1-v-1 to a 2-v-2 situation, and so on, building the numbers and complexity of the games in accordance with the player's skill level and comprehension.

The grid system

When the 2-v-2 situation have been reached, a micro-team game can be formed. The use of a grid system will not only make the organisation of the activities easier, but will create territories in which the games can be played.

The grid may be used by either having it formally marked on the playing area (although in most cases this will be impractical) or, more beneficially, by having it marked off with cones or skittles. (Cones, similar to those used to mark off roadworks, are very useful for this purpose.) The players work within the grids and when ready to play a competitive game, they link up with other grids to create teams and territories.

If this concept is introduced from the beginning it is advantageous to encourage players to create their own games with their own rules and scoring systems. However, players should be led up to this systematically and given tasks that are structured so that a variety of competitive situations are experienced. For example, two players may have been playing competitively on part of a grid (i.e. they are *sharing* that territory and the scoring system may be 'how long a bouncing ball can be kept away from an opponent'). They may then form a 'team' and play against another two players, using the territory of half a grid. The object here would still be to bounce the ball and keep it away from the others, but the criteria for success would be how long the ball is in possession. This task can be developed into two teams of four players sharing a territory (as in most team games), but with goals being introduced, e.g. hoops into which the ball may be bounced. They will now have to try and prevent goals being scored and so a defence system will develop. In these games the numbers must be small so that everyone has a chance to play the ball. The territory should also be kept small to prevent giving too large an area to defend and hence making attack too easy. The territory must be bounded with 'rules' regarding off-side, or out of bounds being introduced, and the goal large enough to allow many scoring possibilities. There must also be a scoring system of some kind, and the score should *always* be checked.

There may be certain activities (e.g. ball volleyed in the air) when the game may be one of a divided territory. Players here need to cooperate to out-manoeuvre those in the opposing territory, thus introducing the idea that cooperation and team work, as well as individual effort, are necessary to successfully play team games.

For older players a different type of defence system may be introduced so that they will sometimes defend the goal itself, i.e. a zone defence, or space marking system, and at other times attach themselves to an individual player to prevent them receiving a pass or scoring a goal, i.e. 'man-to-man' marking.

Gradually the netball territory can be introduced with teams playing on the court, but only using one-third as their territory and playing across the width (Fig. 5).

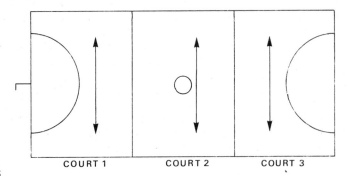

COURT 1   COURT 2   COURT 3

Fig. 5

Teams can be built up from 3-a-side to 5-a-side. They can have positional roles, e.g. Goal Keeper, Centre, Goal Shooter, and have areas of the court in which they can or cannot play. Five-a-side is probably the maximum in such a small space, the positions being Goal Keeper, Wing Defence, Centre, Wing Attack, Goal Shooter. The players can now use centre passes (see ch. 13: *Set Pieces*) and at this stage are ready for a half-court game. In this game, four teams play on one court (see Fig. 6).

The territory is half the full court, and the *scoring system* for the attacking team is by goals scored, and for the defending team by success-fully passing the ball out of the attacking circle back down to the centre

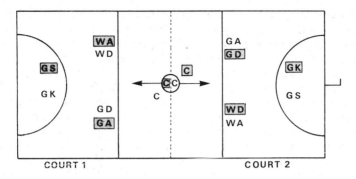

Fig. 6

circle, or the areas on either side. Teams must be changed around so both get a chance to score.

With the half-court game there is more activity for each player than the full 7-a-side game. There is also more opportunity for scoring goals and hence more enjoyment, especially on cold days. When one sees players standing around in the full game (when all the play is at the other end) hardly even getting to touch the ball, and seeing very little in the way of goals, it is hardly surprising that so few enjoy the game sufficiently to wish to continue playing beyond the first years of secondary education.

The full game can be the 'sacred cow' to some coaches and be played at all costs, because of, for instance, the school team. School teams are for the very talented and this type of work is extracurricular—a Netball Club which operates in 'non-timeable' time. During games lessons everyone must be catered for and every lesson afford each an opportunity to develop their skill and experience the enjoyment of playing a game, even if that game is not adult netball. Therefore, at junior school level for instance, playing the full game of netball is not always essential to improving performance; in fact it can be harmful. It is better to work towards improving skills by the use of simple game-like situations.

5
Foot Awareness

The use of feet in netball is most important, not only because an inability to control them leads to an infringement of the footwork rule (see *Official Netball Rules,* A.E.N.A) but because each skill aspect of the game requires a specific use of the feet. Skills, such as setting the body into motion, arresting motion, throwing and shooting, defending and attacking, all require the player to use her feet in a specific way. Players must therefore be given as many opportunities as possible to use a variety of locomotor activities. For example:

1 Running, using different speeds and stride length.

2 Hopping and bounding.

3 Jumping, using different combinations of feet for take-off and landing.

The markings of the court could be used as a 'track' for locomotor activities, e.g: shuttle relays across one-third of the court; running around the outside lines of the court; changing speed at each third line.

SETTING THE BODY INTO MOTION

As players become more adept at using their feet (with older players from the outset), it is important to coach how they may be used in setting the body quickly into motion.

Netball is a game where sharp bursts of speed, e.g. at a centre pass, are essential to gain the initiative over an opponent. The use of the feet for a sprint start in netball is very similar to that used in athletics:

1 The feet are close together so that the body is in an unstable position. This makes the initiation of motion relatively easy.

2 Both feet are pointing in the same direction so that all the force is exerted directly backwards, resulting in the body reacting in a forward direction.

3 The weight is predominantly over the front foot so that it has already been moved into the direction in which the player is intending to move.

4 The knees are flexed, and the muscles of the thighs and hips are used to retain the degree of stability so essential if overbalancing, and breaking the line prior to the whistle, is not to occur.

Contrary to popular belief, the most efficient position for the player to start quickly from is when the heels are in contact with the floor. If the heels are raised, and the weight is on the balls of the feet, the first action of the player on hearing the whistle will be to push back, thus rocking back on the heels and delaying the actual movement forward. Most netball players have been conditioned from the outset to 'keep on the toes', and they may therefore find the flat, starting position rather difficult. If a player genuinely finds this position uncomfortable, it is probably better to sacrifice the slight loss of speed rather than create an uncomfortable starting position.

A tactical consideration is that the player should be able to start equally well with either foot forward so that she can keep her opponent at least a body width behind her, and 'block' her starting position on the line and hence her path to the ball.

Developing the skill

Task One
Players take up a position behind a line bounding an area of the court into which they wish to sprint. The body position they adopt is as described above, and the position of the feet is shown in Figure 7.

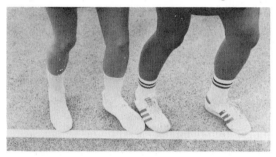

Fig. 7

On the whistle, players sprint off the mark, as fast as possible, for a distance of approximately 15', and then stop (with players who know the foot rule, should use this to stop). They then jog back to the line and repeat in the opposite direction, leading with the other foot.

N.B. Players must not concentrate on the sound of the whistle, but on the movement they are to make. The whistle is a predictable signal which only contains information on when to start or restart a game. The player should therefore only be thinking about her first movement on hearing this signal.

Task Two
Catching a ball should be introduced as soon as possible into this skill. Players work in pairs (A and B), with a ball between them. Player A positions herself as in task one, and Player B positions herself ahead of Player A, who is facing her (see Fig. 8).

To set this skill in motion, Player B tosses the ball in the air and regains possession. As the ball is caught, Player A sprints off the line and runs directly out ahead of Player B, who throws the ball (see Fig. 8). Player A lands, obeying the foot rule, and, if necessary, pivots round to face Player B and passes the ball back to her. Player A then jogs back to the line and

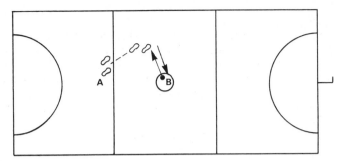

Fig. 8

repeats the movement to the other side, with the other foot leading.

Coaching points
When a player receives a pass in netball she does not usually redistribute the ball to a static player. For this reason the next task is to develop the above skill so that as the receiver lands with the ball the sender moves into a space to receive a return pass.

N.B. If the player receiving the return pass moves too soon, a condition should be introduced so that the receiver will not be able to move until the sender shouts 'now'—when she is ready to throw the ball. Another fault may be that the thrower pivots in a full circle to face the receiver rather than taking the shortest route. This should be corrected as early as possible because, once ingrained, it is a habit which is hard to break and can make the timing of the next receiver's move in the game very difficult.

Fig. 9

Task Three
In a game, the attacking player will usually have an opponent to elude before receiving a pass and, therefore, the next stage is to introduce opposition for the receiver. As the line bounds an 'off-side' area, which is forbidden until the whistle, the players position themselves behind the line (see Fig. 9). The defence can mark either side of her opponent, but, by the quick and skilful use of her feet, the attacker should still have the advantage.

The signal to start play is as above and from this point the skill develops as for task two.

The final stage of this task is to introduce an opponent to the thrower. The player may not double-mark the receiver, but must instead make the first throw more difficult and give the receiver a more realistic target to aim her return pass.

ARRESTING MOTION

In Netball, an arresting motion is a highly specific skill and the footwork rule (see p. 51 and *Official Netball Rules,* A.E.N.A) should be introduced gradually. The advanced player would be able to land efficiently on either foot, but for others it is advisable to teach a right-footed landing for right-handed players, and vice versa.

Netball is a game of short sprints, often with the player having to receive a pass at the end of such a move. The body is travelling very fast on the horizontal plane, and one way to assist in the arresting of this motion is to convert the horizontal motion to a vertical one so that the player jumps to catch the ball before landing.

When setting the body into motion the player's weight must be over the front foot so that she is in a position of being off-balance. In landing, the opposite is necessary; the player, here, needs a stable base so that she is in a balanced position ready to throw the ball and to control her feet.

As the player takes-off and lands, she must come *down* onto the landing foot and, immediately after this foot is grounded, the second foot follows, with short stabbing actions, as a break. If the weight is taken predominantly on the rear foot this means that:

1 There will be less of a chance of contravening the foot rule by dragging the landing foot because the weight is back over the rear foot and would have to travel horizontally forward over the whole base to cause the player to drag the rear foot forwards.

2 The foot will be in the correct position for the player to distribute the ball. However, the width of the base for throwing will depend on the height of the player and the length of pass required. If the player lands with too wide a base, this can be adjusted by movement of the front foot backwards towards the rear, thus narrowing the base to one appropriate to the throwing action. The advanced player should be able to land with the feet

at the correct distance to make the next pass, and should only have to adjust base when overstretched to reach the ball; a process which takes time and allows the defence to position themselves.

Developing the skill

Jumping to land on one foot will help develop the skill and, using the markings of the court (if different coloured markings are available, use these instead), the following task helps to achieve this aim.

Task

The players run freely (the speed of the run depending on their skill) and, on the whistle, run towards the nearest line, jump up and try to land with their right foot (for right-handers) on the line. Players should try to come *down* on the line so that the weight is back. The other foot is used as a break (by taking short, stabbing 'strides').

   With the more advanced group, different coloured lines can be used— (e.g. red, yellow, white)—but if coloured lines are not available, use the sidelines (red); third lines (yellow); circle (shooting and centre) lines (white). On the whistle, the players run towards the nearest line:
— If it is *red,* players land on *right* then *left foot;*
— if it is *yellow* they land on *left* then *right foot;* and
— if it is *white* they land with *both feet simultaneously.*

Coaching point
If players are experiencing difficulty in acquiring this skill, chalk circles of approximately 3′ diameter on the court and get them to run towards a circle, jump off one foot and land on the other inside the circle. The landing foot must remain in the 'circle' while the take-off foot acts as a break outside.

PIVOTING

Often on catching the ball a player has to adjust her foot position so that she can make an efficient distribution of the ball. So often this is made with one long stride, which can be both inefficient and may create an off-balance situation. Pivoting can help alleviate these problems.

Developing the skill

This skill will be improved by:
   1 Players taking their weight on one foot, and lunging out to the side in any direction.
   2 Players using short, pushing steps with the non-weight bearing foot and then returning it to its original position close to the other foot.
   The speed of the *first* push is vital. If it is too slow the whole pivoting action will delay the gaining of an optimum throwing position.

The following task is suggested to further develop this skill:

Task

Working in twos (worker/feeder), with a ball, a 2′ (approx) square is chalked on the court, see Fig. 10.

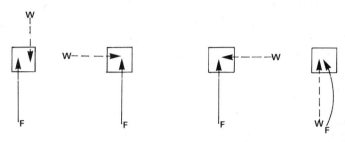

Fig. 10

Feeder puts the ball in play so that the worker receives it and lands, obeying the foot rule, with both feet in the square. The worker can travel to the square: (1) forwards, (2) from right and left, or (3) backwards. The feed must be sympathetic, e.g. a bounce or a chest pass placed ahead of the player. Where the player is travelling backwards, an accurate overhead pass is needed.

Having received the pass and landed, the worker returns the pass to the feeder. No radical adjustment of base should be required because the return pass is short and to a static target. To develop this skill, the feeder, having fed the ball, should now move into the appropriate space to receive or return a pass. In this instance, however, the thrower will need to adjust her base according to the type of pass she is required to make.

The players should work at pushing and pivoting so that they continually adjust the frontal orientation of the body—they should also practise landing on both the right and left foot.

STARTING – STOPPING – PIVOTING

Developing the skill

Task One

Link together the work, already covered above, by getting the players to:
  1 Use a small base and start to sprint in a given direction.
  2 On the whistle signal, jump and land on either foot.
  3 Use the non-weight-bearing foot to adjust their base and pivot their body to face another direction.
  4 Use a small base to sprint out into a new direction. Repeat this move so that the player can start, land and adjust her weight *quickly* with either foot.

As soon as possible add a catching skill to this task by working players in twos (A and B) with a ball:

Player A starts the skill by tossing the ball and recatching it. Player B, starting from a narrow base, sprints out to receive the ball passed ahead of her into the space into which she is moving. As Player B catches and lands, Player A sprints off to receive the return pass. As Player A moves into the space, Player B has to pivot quickly so that she is facing the receiver. This is repeated so that both players have to:

1 Start.
2 Sprint.
3 Catch.
4 Stop.
5 Adjust.
6 Redistribute the ball.

Task Two
Working in threes (A, B and C) with a ball as shown in Figure 11A.

Player A commences the skill with the ball and passes to the space (see Fig. 11 B, C). Player C sprints to receive the ball in the space, lands, adjusts base, and throws into the space she has just left, where Player B sprints and receives the pass. She adjusts base and passes back to the space she has just left, which is now filled by Player A.

Coaching points:
Accuracy of pass is important because it helps the receiver make fewer adjustments of base before passing.

Speed in adjusting base is essential, particularly for the first adjusting movement.

Timing the move of the player, and speed of the ball, is also necessary so that they both arrive simultaneously in the free space.

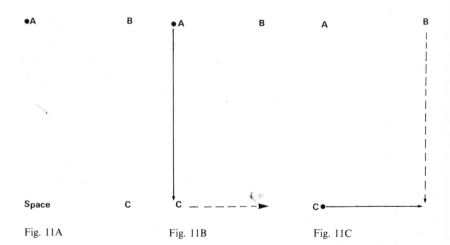

Fig. 11A   Fig. 11B   Fig. 11C

For advanced players only:

Task One

Repeat the above skill, but players take the ball in the air and make a half turn to the right *before* landing, and land in a position to release the ball immediately.

Task Two

Use the whole court with four feeders using a ball each. The number of workers depends on the number in the group, but do not use too many as this will involve too much waiting between activity. Use the court as shown in Figure 12.

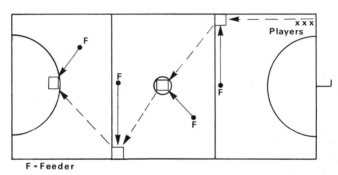

Fig. 12

Mark off squares approximately 2' square. These are marked either just before an area, which could be off-side, or an area (e.g. the goal circle), where it is essential the player lands inside to shoot for goal. (The centre area helps to break up a long run across the whole of the centre third, but with advanced players this can be omitted.) The player starts behind the goal-line and sprints to receive a pass from the first feeder. She must catch the ball in the air and land in the box. *She must not land over the third line.* The ball is then returned to the feeder, whose base should be adjusted quickly so as to speed up the whole action. The player proceeds down the court, as before, and, when she lands in the circle, shoots for goal. Hit or miss she must collect the ball and return it to the feeder for the next player to receive.

Coaching points

Time the pass so that player and ball reach the target simultaneously, and ensure that the base adjustment and pivot are enacted with speed.

The player's movement off the ball is important, i.e. as soon as the ball has been released, they should quickly move onto the next target area.

Task Three

Working in twos with a ball between two, the players position themselves as shown in Figure 13.

The worker starts with feet astride a line but, with a narrow base, has her back to the target area. The feeder passes a high ball overhead in the target

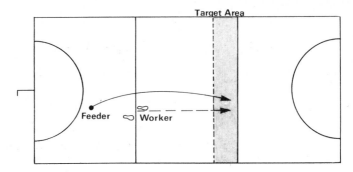

Fig. 13

area, so that the worker has to move back in an efficient way—usually by travelling back having half-turned so she is in a good position to:

1 Move relatively quickly.

2 Jump to receive the ball in the target area.

3 Be aware of both the ball and the target area.

The worker then jumps to catch the ball in the air and lands with both feet in the target area, adjusts base (with advanced players this adjustment should only need to be minimal) and returns the ball to the feeder. The worker sprints back to the starting line, checks with her feet across the line, and the skill continues as before.

This can be made competitive by setting players the task of seeing how many balls they can receive accurately (in the area) within 60 seconds.

N.B. The worker must always return to the starting position before recommencing to move back.

Coaching points.
Encourage players to travel backwards, with small sideways, gathering steps, i.e. the feet not passing each other.

The hips should be over the base so that an efficient jump can be made to receive the ball. For maximum efficiency, the base must be adjusted as quickly as possible.

Ensure speed of movement off the ball for players to return to the starting position.

The feed must be accurate so that ball and player arrive simultaneously. The trajectory should not be so flat that it arrives too quickly, nor so loopy that it drops into the player's hands without having to spring and collect.

As previously stated (p. 26), the use of the feet is specific to each skill area in the game. However, when analysing the basic skills it is suggested that rather than looking at them from the point of view of the use of the feet, each skill be analysed in terms of all relevant components, and emphasis placed on the feet where appropriate.

6
Ball Handling: Receiving

CATCHING

Whenever possible, and certainly in the early stages of learning, catching should be done with two hands. In using one hand to catch the ball the receiver will undoubtedly gain reach because an asymmetric extension allows her to extend beyond that of symmetry. However, one-handed catching is risky, even for the advanced player, and should be only used in an emergency. When the player is forced to take a ball in one hand, she should be encouraged (for security of possession) to quickly get the second hand in contact.

When a ball is caught it gives up a certain amount of the energy it possesses. If the ball is to be brought to rest, the work done by the hands must equal the energy possessed by the ball immediately before it makes contact. In order to do this the player should attempt to increase the distance through which the force acts, i.e. she reaches out to snatch the ball out of the air and pulls it in towards her body.

This action serves other purposes:

1 It decreases the flight-time of the ball through the air. This is advantageous in that time in the air is defence time.

2 It allows the player to attempt to outreach her opponent.

However, a player must beware of keeping the arms extended while gaining possession. In this instance the ball would strike an unyielding surface and possibly rebound off, causing the player to infringe the possession rule (see the *Official Rules of Netball,* A.E.N.A).

Correct timing is essential if this action is to be successful and the player must time not only the extension towards the ball, but also the relaxation of the fingers and the recoil of the arms to pull the ball in towards the body. The use of the hands is obviously vitally important in gaining possession. With beginners it is best to teach that, on receiving the ball, their hands adopt a shape which will reflect the shape of the ball, i.e. a rounded or cupped shape. This shape should be a complete semi-circle (i.e. the thumbs nearly meeting each other to the rear), thus forming a barrier or break to prevent the ball passing directly through the cup.

The hands should be firm, but not stiff and beginners should initially be taught to relax this firmness as the catching sequence begins.

EYE ON THE BALL

Beginners will probably need to keep their eyes on the ball throughout its passage to their hands. The advanced player will not. Experience will have taught her (although probably not at a conscious level) what to expect following the release of a ball at a given speed and height. To concentrate solely on the ball would mean that she will undoubtedly miss other cues so important to the game. She should, of course, always be aware of the position of the ball and, at certain times, place all her attention on it but, for the most part, she should only need to monitor the high spots, i.e. the point of release of the ball and its contact with her hands. She would have caught so many balls in so many different positions that other forms of feedback will be operating and she will be able to quickly turn her visual attention to the distribution of the ball in her possession.

Developing the skill

Task One
The players, with a ball each, toss the ball into the air in front of them and reach out to gain possession. Once they have the pattern established, they should be encouraged to *snatch* the ball out of the air and pull it in towards the centre of the body. One way of getting the players to emphasise their possession of the ball is to get them to shout loudly *'it's mine'* as they snatch it out of the air. To make this task more difficult, the ball may be played into a variety of situations, e.g. behind the body; to either side; high in the air; dropping to the floor; thus players would now have to adjust to different flight paths and speeds. The ball could sometimes be placed out of reach so that players would have to adjust their base to achieve the optimum catching position.

Task Two
Until now, the player has been putting the ball into play by herself, and therefore knows such facts as time and speed of release, and direction of flight. Players must now work in twos, facing each other, about 4' apart. The player with the ball can put it into play in any way she chooses (e.g. high in the air, dropping to the ground, etc). The free player has to snatch the ball out of the air and gain possession, pulling the ball not only into her body, but *away from the opponent.* This skill can be taken either alternately (i.e. that the receiver having gained possession puts it into play for her partner), or that one player is put continuously under pressure.

To make this skill more fun, and also to add a degree of difficulty, the following development may be added.

The players work as above, but this time the receiver turns her back on her opponent, so that she cannot see the ball put into play. The feeder calls *'Play'* and then distributes the ball any way she chooses, e.g. bounced, rolled, high in the air, etc. The receiver has to turn quickly and snatch the ball as fast as possible.

N.B. The receiver should be in a ready position, her base relatively narrow so that she can start to turn as fast as possible to gain her first sight of the ball. Beware of the receiver turning her head so that she is in a position to use her peripheral vision to gain some cue as to the position of the ball and type of pass being used.

Task Three

A further practice to put the stress on the receiver is to have her defending goal in the style of a soccer goalkeeper. Mark out an area of wall, or netting, as the goal. The receiver then stands with her back to the goal, about 2' away from the wall or net. The thrower faces the receiver at a distance that should vary according to the skill level of the players. (In all throwing and catching skills this distance is important. The closer players are, the faster will be the response of the receiver as she will have only a short time in which to assess the relevant cues in the situation.)

The thrower aims to score a goal by getting the ball past the receiver into the net. She may use any pass she chooses, including rolling the ball along the ground. The receiver should adopt a base which affords maximum readiness (i.e. a narrow base) and her weight should be evenly distributed over the balls of her feet. The player may bounce slightly on the spot ready to move in the required direction. Her attention should be on the ball, as all other information in this situation is redundant. Once the receiver has possession of the ball she must obey the foot-rule, adjust her base, pass the ball back to the thrower, and prepare herself for the next pass.

Coaching points

In all of the above skills, the coaching points are very similar:

Eye on the ball: The receiver should be attending to the relevant cues in the display, i.e. watching the ball. With beginners it is essential that this is stressed as they often fail to gain possession because they take their eye 'off the ball'. With experienced players, they may watch for the first movement of the thrower's hands which will be the signal that the ball is to be thrown. However, they too must watch the ball to monitor the level, direction, speed and force of the pass.

Reach: The extension of the arms is vitally important. It is surprising how many netball players reach for a ball with bent elbows. The arms must be fully extended so that, where necessary, the player may outreach an opponent.

Snatch: The speed which the arms are flexed is essential if the ball is to be snatched into the safety of the player's body.

Hands: The shape and degree of tension in the hands and fingers is important. The hands must present a wide, flexible surface into which the ball can be gathered. Young children in particular find this very difficult, and usually present an unyielding surface off which the ball bounces. In this case, stress the lack of sound, i.e. not hearing the ball being caught. Obviously this will mean that the ball will not be snatched vigourously but, in these early stages, accuracy of catching rather than speed should be stressed.

Redistribution: Once the ball is in possession it should be moved as quickly and efficiently as possible into the optimum position for distribution. Where tactically possible the players should always aim to cut down preparation time and speed up the distribution of the ball. However, in any open skill situation, this depends on variables such as the readiness of the next receiver, the position of the defence players, and the degree of control the players have been able to exert initially on the ball.

WHERE TO RECEIVE THE BALL

Generally speaking in netball, the ball is received in the space ahead or above the direction in which the body is moving. For some this may be a difficult concept to grasp. Added to this, in the early stages, it is not easy for the thrower to be able to judge both the correct space and time to place the ball. This next skill is aimed at assisting both thrower and receiver.

Task
The use of the visual cues will help cut down the number of decisions a player has to make, thus leaving her more time to attend to executing the skill. Using the lines of the court, players position themselves as shown in Figure 14A,B,C.

The receiver now has a clear pathway marked out along which she can run to receive the ball. The thrower can see where the receiver is moving, and also has a line which acts as guide for her pass. Ideally, the receiver and

A

B

C

Fig. 14A—C

the ball should meet at an angle of 90°, i.e. the intersection of the two lines in target area X.

The skill can be started by the thrower tossing and regaining possession of the ball, which will be the signal for the receiver to move. However, in this early stage, players are often unable to judge relative speeds, and because (in the skill) the ball is travelling a shorter distance through the air than the player along the ground, the ball will (if both start at the same time) arrive ahead of the player. One way to achieve correct timing is to get the receiver to shout 'now' when she wants the ball. Unfortunately, though, the player may not know when she wants it and, with the fact she now has two things to do at once, this may create an overload situation and cause the skill to break down. The best and possibly easiest way to teach this concept is to tell the thrower to release the ball when the receiver reaches a given point in her run. The task could start at an arbitrary point where players are encouraged to adjust according to the results of their trials.

Coaching points:
The receiver must run along her pathway and increase speed as she reaches the target area. Arms should be extended, elbows straight, and both hands spread around the ball. The ball must be snatched towards the body and, after receiving the ball, the base should be adjusted and the ball thrown back to the feeder.

Depending on the skill level of players, the following factors can be introduced into the above task:

1 Start quickly from the spot.
2 Obey the foot rule on landing.
3 Pivot quickly so that the thrower is faced and the ball passed back.
4 The feeder, having seen the ball safely into the receiver's hands, moves away from the spot so that the player with the ball has to aim at a moving target.
5 Create opposition by first marking the receiver, and then both the receiver and the thrower.

N.B. From Figure 14A,B,C, it can be seen that the receiver's pathway extends beyond the target area. Ensure from the earliest possible time that the player is trained to receive the ball from either side. Once the player has received and distributed the ball, she must move along the pathway beyond the target area and recommence the skill from the other side.

PRESSURE TRAINING FOR RECEIVING THE BALL

Task One: Pepper-Pot
Number of players: 3 (A,B,C)
Number of balls: 2
Position: Triangle shape—stationary (see Fig. 15).

Player A receives the ball from Player B and passes back to her.

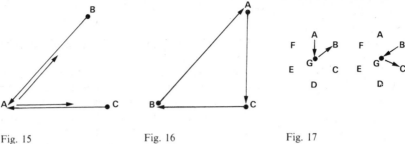

Fig. 15   Fig. 16   Fig. 17

Immediately, Player A receives from Player C and also passes back to her. As Player A becomes more adept at receiving, Players B and C (feeders) must pressurise her by increasing the speed of a pass.

Task Two: Round the Set
Number of players: 3 (A,B,C)
Number of balls: 2
Position: Triangle shape—stationary (see Fig. 16).

The players pass the balls clockwise around the triangle. At any time a given player calls 'change' and the balls are passed anti-clockwise. This can be done with four players and three balls in a square formation.

Task Three: In and Out
Number of players: 6 or 7
Number of balls: 2
Position: A circle with one player (G) in the centre (see Fig. 17). (It is this player who is under pressure.)
The player in the centre (G) passes the ball to Player B and receives from Player A. Player G then passes to Player C and receives from Player B, to then pass to Player D and receive from Player C. Player G then passes to Player E and receives from Player D, to continue around the circle.

Coaching points
The circle should not be too big because the player in the centre must be able to monitor both receiver and thrower by the use of peripheral vision. Also it will take too long for each player to have a turn.

Change the player in the centre when the skill starts to break down. This is rather an intense practice; plus moving in the circle can make the player feel dizzy.

The player in the centre should use a pivoting action of the feet to keep a continuous movement around the circle.

N.B. As this is a very static practice for those in the circle, *do not* introduce it on cold days.

Task Four: Keeping Goal
Number of players: 3 (A,B,C)
Number of balls: 2
Position: Player A faces Players B and C in a 'goal' marked-off on the wall/net.

As with the 'goalkeeper practice' described on p. 111, the player in goal has to keep the ball out of the net. The other two keep a constant stream of balls coming at her at varying heights, speeds and forces of delivery.

Player A in goal must adopt a mobile base, and her attention should switch between the balls being put in by the two feeders (Players B and C). She should attempt to gain possession of every ball aimed at the goal. If she cannot gain clean possession, she should attempt to clear the ball from the goal area and back to the thrower.

Task Five: Two Ball Square
Number of players: 5 (A-E)
Number of balls: 2
Position: A square with one player (E) in the centre (see Fig. 18.)

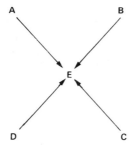

Fig. 18

Player B passes to Player E who passes to Player A and *immediately* receives from Player C and passes to Player D. The balls should continue around the square, via the centre, thus putting the player in the centre under pressure.

Coaching points
Player E must have the ability to make half-turns to either left or right, and be able to pivot taking the weight on either foot. The speed of this practice will involve a very speedy change of feet.

Player E must also be able to switch her attention quickly from one ball to the next.

7
Ball Handling: Distribution

A good pass is that which arrives at the right player, in the right space, at the right time. There has in the past been a tendency to categorise the various throwing actions used in the game into the five basic passes. What is proposed here is a simpler classification, based on the principles which underlie all throwing actions. Namely, that there are two types of pass: those made with two hands and those with one.

Passing and shooting allow wide scope for individual flair and inventiveness, and, in an open skill situation, deception of an opponent is part of the overall aim. In netball, a throw and a shot may be defended by the opposition and, therefore, the greater facility a player has for disguising her true intention, the greater are her chances of success. For this reason the coach should be prepared to accept the idiosyncratic or unorthodox. However, it must be stressed that the above are only acceptable when they are part of a player's skill repertoire and can be repeated successfully. Unorthodox actions are only acceptable if the coach feels they will not prevent the development of the player's skill; or be quickly analysed and capitalized upon by the opposition. There are no hard and fast rules here and it is a matter for the individual coach to decide when to try and coach out unorthodox actions. What the coach is aiming to develop in her players is a flexible response based on the understanding of sound principles.

PASSING

The objective of passing is to complete a successful passage of the ball between the hands of one player, and the hands of a predetermined team mate; this involves the passage of the ball (to the selected player) either through the air or via the floor.

Flight path of the ball

In passing, the flight of the ball is governed by:
1 The velocity of release.
2 The angle of release.
3 Air resistance.
4 Spin.

Velocity
This is governed by the force exerted on the ball, i.e. the muscular force. In netball, any pass may be defended and therefore it is almost always essential to make the pass as quickly as possible. Therefore, those muscular forces which can act most quickly should be utilised. These are the muscle

groups producing flexion of elbow, wrist and fingers. Only when these forces are insufficient, i.e. when the ball has to travel over a considerable distance, do the slower moving, but more powerful muscles of the trunk and legs have to be used.

Angle of release

This will depend on (1) the height of the receiver and her opponent, (2) the throwers own opponent, (3) the space the receiver has available in which to move, and (4) the speed at which she is moving. The angle of release is determined by the point from which the player distributes the ball. Generally speaking, if the ball is released early in the action, it will go high, and if released late it will have a dropping flight path.

Air resistance or drag

This has little significance in this skill.

Spin

When a player throws a ball she invariably imparts spin. In the majority of cases this is back-spin which, as a result of gravity, tends to slow the rate at which the ball falls. Provided the back-spin is not so great that it provides difficulties for the catcher, it is advantageous in that it enables the ball to follow a slightly more direct path than would otherwise be possible. Side-spin and top-spin are not often used except in a bounce pass when the very skilful player can use them to assist in producing the desired effect.

Foot awareness in throwing

As previously stated above, it is the fast moving muscle groups of the hand, arm and shoulder girdle which primarily contribute to fast and accurate distribution of the ball. If the players are relatively near to each other, then the arms alone will be sufficient for efficient distribution. However, two points should be noted here. Firstly, the player is often in a position to have to make a long, hard pass which requires considerable muscular force, harnessed by correct timing. Secondly, most females are not strong in the hand, arm and shoulder muscles. For these reasons the player very often has to utilise the stronger, but slower muscles of the trunk and legs. It may seem strange to say that when a player's passing is poor it might be as well to look at her feet to find the reason for this short-fall.

When teaching the footwork rule (p. 51) it was suggested that the employment of a right-footed landing for a right-handed player ensured that she had the most efficient base from which to throw. It is so often the placement of the feet which causes the player to produce a weak or inefficient throw. To illustrate this point, the throwing action is examined below.

THE THROWING ACTION ANALYSED

The throwing action involves total body activity. It would be incorrect to say that players require great strength in their muscles to achieve a powerful and efficient throwing action, but it undoubtedly helps. It is strength, allied to balance and correct timing, which will achieve a high level skill in throwing. The following factors are also helpful in attaining a well-executed throw:

1 The foot corresponding to the dominant hand should be to the rear.

2 The width of the base is dictated by the height and strength of the player, and the distance over which she has to throw. A small player will need a narrower base than a tall player. If the ball has to travel a long distance, the wider base will give a greater time for the forces to act.

3 The feet should be pointing in the direction of the throw. Players are often very careless about foot placement and adopt inefficient throwing bases with feet turned out, or the front foot placed *directly* in front of the rear.

4 The preparation with the ball will again depend on the distance it has to travel. Generally speaking, the longer the throw the longer the preparation required. However, this preparation should not be such that its length and slowness 'telegraphs' the throwers intention to the opposition.

5 Grip—the ball may be held in one hand or two. As a rule, two hands are more secure and, even if a one-handed pass is to be executed, the other hand should be used as a support until the throwing action is begun.

6 As the muscles of the trunk and legs are slower, they will start moving first and the player will therefore either step onto the front foot, or transfer the weight of the body over the front foot *before* the ball is released.

7 If the ball has received an asymmetric preparation, the shoulders will have twisted around the hips which will have remained relatively fixed. The unwinding of this twist contributes to the force applied to the ball. From the preparatory position, which may be close to the chest, just behind either shoulder, or overhead, the arms extend and the hands release the ball. The actual point of release dictates the ball's flight path.

8 After the ball is released, the weight of the body continues following through over the front foot. The arms and hands extend in the direction of the flight of the ball. The trunk should remain stable and not bend too much at the waist so as to cause the player to fall away to that side and skew the flight of the ball in a sideways and downwards direction.

The two categories of throw suggested here are that the player either releases the ball using one of two hands. The factors, which make each pass significantly different from the rest, are the preparation and the point of release.

The throwing preparation of the player may be either symmetrical, or asymmetrical (i.e in front of, above, or to the side of the body). The point of release may occur at different points on the arc of preparation. This aspect is vitally important because where the ball is released dictates whether the ball goes in a high loop over the head of a defence, rebounds off the floor, or goes in a direct line to the player. Speaking generally, an early release of the ball will result in a rising flight path, while the longer the release is

Table 1   Classification of throwing actions—both hands

Preparation	Point of release	Level of release	Speed of release	Result
In front of the body	At full extension of the arms directly ahead	Chest level just above the horizontal	Fast with finger and wrist snap	Chest pass
In front of the body	At full extension of the arms directed downwards	Low, below waist level	Fast, often with back, top, or side spin	Bounce
Away from the body symmetrically overhead	Early, arms still flexed	High, just behind the head	Slow	High lob
Away from the body symmetrically overhead	As the arms are extending the follow through is cut down	Just above or slightly forward of head	Fast, with finger and wrist snap	Two-handed overhead
Away from the body symmetrically to either side	As arms are extending	Just behind or in line with the shoulder	Fast with finger and wrist snap	Two-handed shoulder

delayed, the lower the ball's flight will be. To make this concept more readily understandable, see Table 1.

A similar form of analysis can be done for the one-handed passes (see Table 2). One-handed passes are more risky than their two-handed equivalents, but two important passes, which are made essentially with one hand (i.e. the underarm pass, and the one-handed shoulder or javelin pass) are worth similar analysis.

Table 2   Classification of throwing actions—one-handed

Preparation	Point of release	Level of release	Speed of release	Result
Asymmetric away from the body— low	Early in the arc of the arm swing *or* (Depending on the angle of release required) Late in the swing	Waist level	Fast	Scoop or underarm pass
Asymmetric away from the body —high	As the arm passes the line of the body.	Head level	Fast	Shoulder or javelin

TECHNIQUES OF THROWING

In order to assist the coach to evaluate performance by an analysis of skill, the techniques of certain, specific throws are outlined here.

The chest pass

The ball should be supported in two hands at chest height, with the thumbs pointing towards each other with the fingers comfortably spread behind the ball. The ball is then drawn slightly back as the wrists are 'cocked', before applying force to the ball in the direction of the pass. (The cocking of the wrists places them in such a position that the muscles, which flex the wrist, can exert force over a longer distance and thus do more work on the ball than would otherwise be possible). The cocking of the wrists should then be immediately followed by a coordinated series of actions in which the elbows are extended and the wrists and fingers are rapidly flexed or snapped to apply force to the ball.

The above arm action is frequently accompanied by a step forward and possibly a lifting of the body weight in the direction of the throw. This pass is normally directed so that the ball is caught between waist and shoulder level, although the point of release will dictate its flight path.

The overhead pass

The ball is held in two hands either:

1 Directly above the head.
2 Slightly forward of the head.
3 Just to the rear of the head.

The exact position depends on the angle of release required. The fingers are spread pointing upwards and the thumbs directed towards each other. The elbows are flexed and kept pointed outwards, and the ball is propelled away with a quick, forceful flexion of the wrists and fingers. The weight is often moved onto and over the front foot. As most force comes from the wrists and fingers, the follow-through is limited, but elbows will extend.

For tactical reasons, some overhead passes will need an early point of release so that the ball is lifted over the heads of the defence. The normal two-handed overhead pass, however, is released in front of the head and travels fast and direct to the receiver.

The bounce pass

This is a most useful pass and is not used nearly enough in netball. Granted, it takes longer to make because it has to rebound off a second surface (i.e. the floor) before it reaches the receiver, but it is a very useful pass in a congested space, or to pass a tall defence.

This pass can be made with one or two hands. The grip for the two-handed pass is the same as for the chest pass. The ball is directed towards the floor in such a manner that it strikes the floor either:

1 Just behind the feet of a 'tight' defender.
2 Approximately two-thirds of the way between sender and receiver.

Spin is important in the bounce pass and this can be stated as:
1 Top spin = increased distance.
2 Back spin = make the ball sit up into the receiver's hand.
3 Side spin = swerve to evade a defence.
Because the speed is reduced by contact with the floor, greater force is required in the bounce pass, and this is usually obtained by stepping forward into the direction of the bounce.

The one-handed shoulder pass (right handed)
The ball is raised above and to the rear of the right shoulder. The fingers are spread and pointing upwards, the palm cupped and the thumbs spread laterally to provide a support for the ball. The base is *approximately* shoulder width, but this will vary according to the distance required in the throw. The base may be taken after receiving the ball, or the player may step forwards before the ball is released. The hips rotate and shoulders rotate to the side, and both should rotate forwards during the throw, with the full force imparted to the ball.

Following the rotation of shoulders and hips, there is a coordinated extension of upper arm elbow, forearm, wrists and fingers in the direction in which the ball is being sent. The ball is released at, or slightly above, head height just as the hand passes through the vertical plane.

Follow-through is accomplished by the weight passing over the front foot and possibly continuing into a stepwise action. The arm and hand follow through in the arc of swing and returns to assist normal body balance.

Developing the skill

As with all skills the following formula should be adopted:
1 *Introduce* the skill in an unpressurized and usually static situation.
2 *Increase the complexity* and realism by introducing movement of one or other and eventually both players.
3 Make the skill *competitive* — How many?
How long?
4 Introduce *opposition* and create a realistic game situation.

Where the skill of throwing is concerned, there is obviously going to be a fair amount of static work, both in the early days and when breaking down and analysing the skill with players. However, static work should be kept to a minimum, and while the player is generally static when throwing the ball she rarely throws to a static target. It must be remembered that two players standing still and throwing the ball to each other is very different to the skill of throwing used in the game.

In order to introduce the basic principles of throwing, the two players stand facing each other about 12″ apart with a ball between them. The ball is then thrown, using two hands, and after the throw is completed the player takes one step away from her partner. The players should continue to do this noticing:
1 When they find it difficult to make the pass using arms only.

2 What they do with their feet to help their arms.

3 Where the ball might start if it has to travel a relatively long distance.

When the players reach the spatial limits of their ability to pass the ball, they should take one step towards their partner after each pass, returning to their starting positions.

The players should repeat the above, being asked to look at *one aspect* each time. In this way it is possible to highlight the basic principles underlying all throws. Once these principles have been grasped, a more specific throwing action can be introduced to players (one at a time).

It is not within the scope of this book for each specific pass to be discussed in terms of the development of skill. However, the formula outlined in chapter 4 can be applied successfully to any specific throw being introduced. The following tasks are for a two-handed pass at chest level:

Task One

Two players with one ball passed statically between them. Do not make the distance between them too narrow or the receiver will not have sufficient time to monitor the relevant cues. Players must be asked to concentrate on one aspect of the skill at a time. Some slight form of competition can be introduced by seeing how many successful passes can be made in a given period of time.

Increase Complexity by introducing movement into the skill. This can be done by using the same skill used in catching (i.e. the players are given visual cues to guide the line of the receiver and the line the ball must follow to reach the receiver.

In this skill, one player remains static and acts as a feeder for the worker. To develop this, both players could move successively to receive a pass. This adds two further degrees of complexity to the task:

1 Movement off the ball.

2 Timing of the move to receive the pass.

While most emphasis must still lay on the skill being coached (i.e. the throw) a shortfall in these other two areas will decrease the efficiency of the performance. The coach should therefore remind the players of the spatial patterning of the previous skill and get them to adjust their position off the ball so that they can move at an angle to the thrower to receive the pass.

N.B. At this early stage, encourage players *not* to move away from the ball as this increase in distance between the sender and receiver creates problems with which the thrower has to cope. If the timing of the movement to receive the pass is very poor, the receiver could be made to stand still until the thrower shouts 'go' and only then may she move for the pass.

Coaching points

The use of the feet. Is the base an appropriate size, well-balanced and pointing in the correct direction?

The use of the arms and hands. How do they prepare the throw, and where do they release the ball?

The follow-through. Do the hands and arms follow the flight of the ball? Do the feet remain glued to the ground and create an off-balance situation, or follow-through into a natural step-wise action?

N.B. A further increase in complexity can be achieved by adding a third player. This means that the receiver is catching a ball thrown by two different people with an obvious variety of styles. This also helps to emphasise the use of space.

Task Two: Fill the Gap
   Number of players: 3 (A,B,C).
   Number of balls: 1
   Positions: As shown in Figure 19.

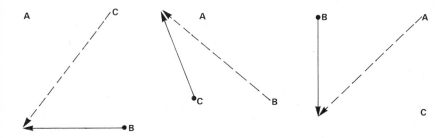

Fig. 19

Player C moves through the gap/space made by the other two players and receives a pass from Player B. A space now exists between herself and Player A. Player B moves through this gap and receives the ball from Player C.

This task repeated with each player filling the gap which exists between the two other players and receiving a pass from one of them. Count how many successful passes are made.

Coaching points
Passing should be into the space ahead of the moving player, and they should not move into the space too soon.

After receiving the ball, the base should be quickly and efficiently adjusted to enable an accurate pass to be made to the succeeding player. As the players will all be moving in one direction, there will come a time when one player has to move successively, i.e. back along the path she has just taken. This will reverse the movement and change the direction in which the skill is moving.

Task Three: Competition
   Number of players: 4 (A–D)

Number of balls: 1—the ball always goes the same way through the sequence.

1 Count how many accurate passes can be made before the skill breaks down;

2 Four consecutive passes = 1 point.

3 Pressure should be put on one player so that the sequence runs:

A to B	C to A
B to A	A to D
A to C	D to A

4 Divide players into a 2-v-2 game situation. The area should be limited with players now using the skill in relatively realistic game-like situations with each pass being defended.

Coaching points

Stress that a pass may have to be adapted to deal with the presence of two opponents. Do not make the area of play too wide as it will make the defence's job too difficult.

The above skills can be taken using one specific type of pass. However, once the players have an enlarged repertoire of passes, the following skills may be added:

Task Four

Number of players: 4 (A–D)

Number of balls: 1

The ball is passed from Player A to D, successively, but each pass must be different from the one which the player received. This means that the. receiver must also be aware of the pass which was made prior to her move, in that she must make her move such that it will assist the thrower to make an appropriate pass.

Task Five

Number of players: 4

Number of balls: 1

The skill proceeds as above, but this time the receiver calls for the type of pass she wants to receive, e.g. high, bounce, chest, etc. Again she must judge her distance as she cannot call, for example, for a bounce pass if she is a considerable distance from the thrower.

Task Six: Instant feedback

Number of players: 4 (A–D).

Number of balls: 1

The ball is passed from player A to D, successively. Players are free to make whichever pass they consider appropriate. The receiver gives the thrower an instant feedback by shouting 'inaccurate' if the pass was not made to her advantage.

N.B. In this skill the receiver should give an indication with a hand to exactly where she wishes to receive a ball.

Task Seven: Break the code
Number of players: 4
Number of balls: 1
Sequence of passes: 4 successively.
The four players make up a code of passes. This code may be based on a rhythm, e.g.:
fast—fast—slow—slow—fast,
on levels high—low—high—low,
of handed passes, e.g. two—two—one—two—two.
Once the group have established their code, they should stop working to indicate they are ready. The group is then divided up so that one observes another *and without discussion* tries to break their code. When they feel they know what it is, they repeat it through. Only when they have done so, do they get feedback from the original group as to how successful they have been.

This is a very useful skill for training observation. Every player should be encouraged from the outset to observe both the players in her own team and the opposition. They should each know such facts as handedness, preferred speed, preferred pass, and the rhythm a player likes to move at. Once these facts are known they can be used to strengthen the cohesiveness of a teams play, and to break down the skills and tactics of the opposition.

Realism

It is absolutely essential that when specific throws are being coached they are made to operate in an area of the game where they are most often used. For this reason the coach should put specific throws under pressure in set pieces (see ch. 13) taken from the game. Examples of this are:

1 A high floating lob from the edge of a circle fed into the shooters.

2 A long diagonal shoulder pass to a player, e.g. Wing Attack or Centre moving away from the thrower into either attacking corner.

3 A chest pass at centre pass.

4 A two-handed overhead from Centre to Wing Attack travelling towards the limits of her area.

5 A bounce pass either into the circle or at a throw-in.

This type of work *must* be done. Firstly, it links the skills with the full game and, secondly, it helps to heighten the understanding of the players. It should also programme them to select the right pass to suit a given situation without having to take too much time to think.

TAKING THE BALL ON THE RUN

The footwork rule of netball permits the player to receive the ball and continue her movements:

The footwork rule
A player may jump to catch and land on one foot. They may then jump

from the landing foot onto the other foot and jump again, but *must throw the ball or shoot before regrounding either foot.*

This is a relatively difficult skill and to use it efficiently requires (1) a high degree of bodily control on the part of the player with the ball, and (2) accurate timing on the part of the receiver. For this reason it is advocated here that it should only be taught when basic footwork has been thoroughly internalised by the players. This skill can be developed further by the use of tasks such as those set out below.

Task One
In 3's with one ball between the three players, who position themselves as shown in Figure 20.

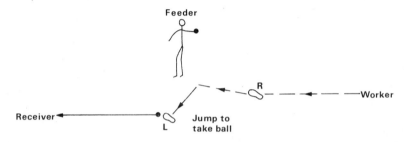

Fig. 20

The feeder stands with the ball held in one hand with her arm extended upwards and forwards. The worker runs towards the feeder, takes off from either foot and jumps at the same time lifting the ball out of the feeder's hand. The worker lands on her opposite foot and, as she moves forward, throws the ball to the receiver *before* re-grounding her take-off foot.

N.B. In this early stage the feeder does *not* throw the ball, as the variations in the throw may add a further complication to the worker's already difficult task.

Task Two
The above skill is repeated, but this time the feeder tips the ball off her hand as the worker approaches. The timing of this may be difficult at first, but all she is being asked to do is flick the ball off her hand as the worker takes off.

Task Three
The final task added to the above is to have the receiver move off the spot and indicate where she wants the ball. Initially she should move in a regular pattern of alternating right and left moves. However, once the worker is used to passing to a moving body, the receiver must make her moves at random. With advanced players, opposition may be put in against the receiver, thus making her timing more realistic. When the players are adept at controlling their feet in this way, the feeder throws the ball to the worker, and the skill proceeds as before.

Task Four

This task may be performed by a large number of players with few balls. The starting position is as shown in Figure 20, but in this case there are two feeders and one worker (i.e. Receiver is now feeder no. 2).

The worker lands on the move—passes to feeder No. 2—who holds up the ball similarly for the worker to run on and take the ball off her hand. The feeders are spaced out so that there are long and short gaps between them.

The players therefore have to adjust their passes according to the space, and will also have to adjust the speed and length of their running stride to suit the distance to the next feeder.

N.B. In order that this skill can progress, a ball should be put into play to feeder no. 1, from the worker—before she starts to move.

Coaching points

All above tasks must be practised in situations which are as realistic to the game as possible. For example:

1 Shooters should practise taking penalty shots on the run.

2 Centre passes to the Wing Defence, who takes the ball on the move and passes on to Wing Attack.

3 A Centre linking Wing Defence and Wing Attack by a fast break across the centre-third.

However, again it must be stressed that for passing to be well-executed a high degree of control and understanding on the part of the players is required. Merely taking the ball on the move is relatively simple but, unless there is close cooperation between players, it can result in uncontrolled play where a player puts herself in the position of either having to get rid of the ball irrespective of the succeeding player's position, or infringe the footwork rule.

8
Shooting

It is very surprising and disturbing to consider how little the skill of shooting is actually taught. It appears (according to netball mythology) that shooters are born and not made. However, while it does seem that certain players do have a definite talent for shooting skills, which earmarks them to play these positions, it might be that if the skill was correctly taught from the outset there may not be so few top-class shooters.

ANALYSIS OF SHOOTING

The objective in shooting is to complete the accurate displacement of the ball from the hands of the shooter through the ring net. Shooting is perhaps the most individualistic of all skills, and any technique which consistently succeeds in getting the ball past the defence and into the net is a good technique. However, there are certain basic principles from which to work:

Base
The player's base, for the static or set shot, is normally narrow although it should be one which will be wide enough to ensure she is well-balanced. As opposed to the throwing action, when shooting, a player normally stands with a forward foot that corresponds to her dominant hand, e.g. right hand/right foot. This is because the shooting action does not require power, but precision.

Support
The ball may be held in one or two hands, but normally the dominant hand supports the ball (i.e. the launching pad) while the other acts as a stabilizer on its rear.

The wrist is cocked and the ball supported on the base of the fingers. The fingers should be well-spread on the rear of the ball, with the thumbs and the little finger affording lateral support.

The forearm is held straight on the vertical plane with the elbow directly under the hand. Once the decision about the distance between hand and ring has been made it should not be altered until the actual shooting action begins (see Fig 21 A-C).

Focus
The focus of attention is on the ring, usually the point on the ring furthest from the shooter.

Preparation
Depending on the distance of the shooter from the ring, and the height and reach of the defence, the shooter commences action with a flexion of the

Fig. 21A—C

A B C

knees. She continues this push directly up through the body. This bodily action takes some of the strain from the shooting arm, whose job is precision.

Fig. 22

Release
The ball is projected away high, with a full extension of the arm and a 'wrist-snap' (as if the player was waving goodbye to the ball). The fingers relax as the ball is released and follow-through in a downward direction (see Figure 22.)

Result
The ball is usually delivered with spin, and should have a sufficiently high trajectory to evade the defence and arrive over the ring. The perfect shot would drop directly through the ring. However, the ball often hits the rear of the ring where, if the spin imparted is a back-spin, the ball drops back into the ring.

The player follows through, as in any throwing action, transferring the weight over the front foot, the rear foot coming through to the front. However, because of the rules governing personal contact, the shooter must control her follow-through so that she avoids the player defending her shot. Also, for this reason, any attempt to follow-up her missed shot must involve the avoidance of the defence.

Developing the shooting skill
Players should be set the task of finding the spot in the circle from which they *cannot miss*. If this is done in the player's own time it is advisable to give them a diagram of the circle drawn to scale and marked out in 1' squares (see Figure 23.)

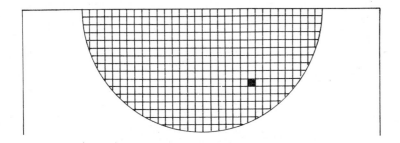

Fig. 23

After a period of experiment, the player marks the square where she has achieved most success. While players are experimenting, they should be asked to consider their:
— base
— support of the ball
— focus of ring
— preparation
— release
— follow-through.

Shooting is partly a question of confidence and once a player feels she can shoot successfully, she is ready to progress. The coach, having verbally analysed the skill with the player working practically, should encourage the player to practise set shots from other points in the circle.

As the shooter does not start with the ball in her possession (except in the case of a penalty shot), the player moves freely in the circle putting the ball into play for herself in a variety of ways, e.g. roll, bounce, toss in the air. She collects the ball, obeys the foot rule, adjusts her base, and shoots. She follows up her shot and, having collected it, recommences the skill.

The player now receives the ball from a feeder outside the circle, e.g. Centre or Wing Attack. She varies (1) how she moves for the ball, e.g. dodge, sprint, block, and (2) the position she receives the ball. The feeder varies the pass she makes, e.g. lob, bounce, chest, etc. Having collected the ball the shooter lands, obeying the foot rule, adjusts her base, shoots and collects the ball.

The next stage here is to put the shooter against opposition. The feeder now has the position of the shooter's opponent to consider in making her pass. The shooter should attempt to manoeuvre her position so that she receives the ball in an area of the circle where she knows she is accurate. This means she must be thinking ahead and constantly adjusting her position in relation to that of the defence so that she can increase her chances of achieving this objective. The feeder varies the position around the circle from which she makes the pass.

PRESSURE TRAINING

Task One
Chalk numbers 1–12, at random, in the circle (see Fig. 24.)

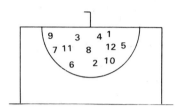

Fig. 24

The shooter starts from number 1. She shoots for goal and, hit or miss, retrieves her own shot, moves to number 2, and so on through the 12 numbers. There are two ways of proceeding with this training (in both instances the players are timed):

1 The player remains at the same number until she scores. Here, the player will obviously take much longer to score 12 goals.

2 Hit or miss she moves on; there will be fewer goals in a faster time.

Task Two
Place skipping ropes at random in the circle. The shooter does 20 fast skips and takes a shot at goal (the skips should be as those used by boxers in training). Hit or miss she collects her own ball, moves to the next rope and continues 20 fast skips, one shot for goal. In this skill, as with task one above, the other variation is that the shooter continues to shoot from a given spot until she is successful.

Task Three
The shooter starts with the ball at position 1 in the inner circle (Fig. 25).

She shoots from this spot until she scores. She then moves to position 2 and repeats and continues on a semi-circular pathway, working gradually further away from the post, until she has covered the whole circle.

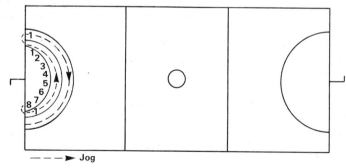

- - - ► **Jog**

Fig. 25

WARM-UP, USING A SHOT FOR GOAL

This is taken from a similar skill used in basketball. In terms of territorial divisions it has no validity, but this is acceptable because it is merely used as a warm-up (see also ch. 12 for further conditions of warm-up).

Task
The players start as shown in Figure 26.

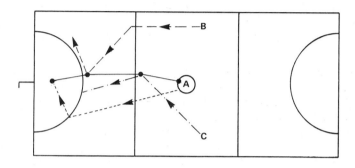

Fig. 26

Three players line up parallel to each other across the width of the court at about centre circle.

Player A is in the centre circle with the ball. Player C is on her left and then sprints diagonally ahead of Player A to receive a direct pass. As Player C sprints, Player B jogs down the court and then sprints directly across the court to a point on the crown of the circle—and receives a direct pass.

Player A then moves out to the side of the court, from which Player C started, and moves from outside into the circle and receives a pass from Player B, and shoots for goal. Player B and C back-up the circle. The players return *down the side of the court* while other groups of players are working.

In this activity it is possible to occupy at least six groups of three players; three groups working towards one goal circle and three groups towards the other.

As can be seen from Figure 26, the players have:
1 Interchanged positions laterally across the court.
2 Changed speed.
3 Changed floor pattern.
4 All taken turns to finish in the circle and shoot for goal, i.e. all players have started with the ball.

SHOOTING ON THE RUN

As with 'passing while on the move' it is possible to shoot while moving.

The development of this skill is done virtually the same way as the throwing skill (see ch. 7) and below are some relevant tasks to achieve this end.

Task One
Player alone with the ball. As in the previous task, the shooter puts the ball into play herself, takes it on the run and shoots (Figure 27 A–C). Hit or miss she collects the ball and starts again.

A

Fig. 27A—C

C

The feeder stands as shown in Figure 28.

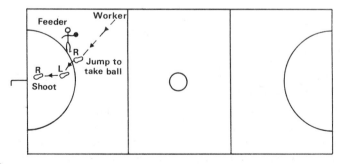

Fig. 28

The worker moves in, taking-off from one foot, lifts the ball from the hand, lands on her other foot, and then takes off from that foot and shoots and lands.

N.B. The skill can be further developed by the feeder tossing the ball off her hand as in the throwing skill; the shooter collecting it and moving on to shoot. The feeder throws the ball from outside the circle—to the shooter moving towards the post inside the circle. The final stage is to feed the shooter, who is now defended, and the activity is now realistic in game terms.

Pressure training

Place skittles in the circle (space about 8′ apart) as shown in Figure 29.

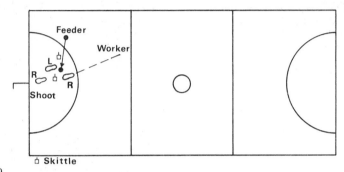

Fig. 29

Feeder passes in from outside. Worker takes-off, receives the pass, makes her step around the skittle and moves in for goal, completing her shot and obeying the foot rule.

The skittles can be placed so that the worker moves not only forward, but steps sideways and then shoots for goal.

STEP-UP PENALTIES

Here the shooter starts statically with the ball in her hand. She steps forward onto one foot, takes-off and shoots for goals when she reaches her high point, and lands.

The shooter should practise step-back shots to operate in those situations where her forward pathway is blocked by a defence, or the frontal position of the defence is creating problems for her shooting action.

N.B. When players are shooting on the move they should remember that, as the body is moving forwards and upwards, there will be less activity in the arm region. Too much of a push from the arms will result in an overshoot. However, the relaxation of the fingers and the wrist flexion is still an integral part of the action, and should be adhered to.

TACTICS

Shooter and Goal Attack must work with each other to gain a sympathetic understanding of each others strengths and weaknesses, but how they play depends on a number of things. For example, a fast, small Goal Attack may make herself into a third attacking feeder, whose job is to give an accurate feed to the Shooter who shoots. If both players are equally accurate they may divide the circle between them (on either side or front and back), depending on where they are most accurate. They should know where each prefers to play and endeavour to create space for each other to operate in their preferred area, (see ch. 11 for more detailed information on tactics).

When Goal Shooter is having a bad day, she should be prepared to move out and create space thus changing roles (but not positions) with the Goal Attack who moves in to do most of the shooting. Whether or not shooters pass within a circle depends upon:

1 Their positions in relation to the goal post, and how accurately they are shooting.

2 The positions of their defences.

3 The degree of attention and awareness that exists between the two shooters, plus that of their opponents.

If the shooter passes the ball out of the circle, and re-positions for her shot, the coach should ensure that she only does this when the second position takes her to a *more advantageous* shooting position.

As a general rule, whenever possible *shoot for goal*

ONE GOAL AT A TIME!

Shooters should be trained that once they have the ball in the circle they should try to blot out everything except their concentration on the ring. This one shooting chance is all that matters. Previous bad shots are forgotten and the necessity for the goal put aside. All she must now concentrate on is *getting this goal—now*.

The shooter's task can (in one way) be relatively easy once they have the ball. They are aiming at a static, albeit small target; and they have three seconds to complete their action. The skill itself is relatively closed and only the position and activity of the defence creates difficulties and makes the skill more open. The shooter may then have to adapt her skill very quickly to cope with this external factor, but, nevertheless, the skill is not as difficult as some others in the game. What is difficult for shooters is pressure. Unless they can get the ball through the ring, their team cannot win. It can be soul-destroying for defences to win a ball, for centre court to take down and feed it into the circle, only to have to defend back and attempt to regain possession after a missed shot.

Once a shooter starts to miss, she may lose her confidence, but not her skill. What the coach (or captain) must try to do in this situation is restore her confidence in her own ability and remind her: *one goal at a time.*

9
Attack

Attack and Defence can be considered as an individual or team skill and this chapter examines the attacking skills in netball (see ch. 10 for defence).

INDIVIDUAL ATTACKING SKILLS

An individual, before she can contribute to the efforts of the team, must be aware of the general principles which govern her own attacking manoeuvres.

Assessing opponent

The important thing is to find the opponent's weakness. The attacker should be encouraged to try a variety of moves so she can discover her opponent's preferences. For example, she may find that her opponent prefers to catch the ball with her right hand. Having observed this, the attacker may endeavour to force the defending player into a position of disadvantage (i.e. she makes her dodge to her opponent's weaker catching side).

Attacks are often initiated by a reaction to cues received from the defensive position; and the defender's attitude and degree of concentration. In order to take full advantage of this, the attacker must concentrate so that any momentary positions of defensive disadvantage are instantly recognised and responded to without hesitation. With practise and experience, players will react more quickly, in various situations, with less input information. One factor which separates the experienced player from the novice is that the experienced will react to slight clues without having to wait to see the entire movement unfold.

Self-assessment

An attacker must attempt to capitalize on her strengths. A Wing Attack, who knows she is very fast off-the-mark, would probably be wise to use a straight sprint for the centre pass. However, this does not mean that she should rely solely on her speed, because one day she will probably meet a Wing Defence who is equally as fast. Every player must work to increase her repertoire of moves so she has the answer to every question the defender may pose. It is a foolish and arrogant player who thinks that all her team-mates will play around her 'single move'. On the other hand, it is equally wasteful not to make full use of an individual's particular expertise.

Timing the move

A good attacker normally moves before a defender is prepared for action. However, even if a defender is ready and alert, the well-timed dodge will usually be successful. Thus, timing is a crucial element both in the beginner's game and in an International match. It is vital that the attacker has the patience to wait, because if she moves too soon she may well get 'trapped' by the defender. The mistake many attackers make is that they move immediately a team-mate catches the ball. This is the wrong cue for action because the player still has to land and balance before she is ready to throw. Obviously the time for the transition from catching to throwing is reduced as the player becomes more skilful.

Moving off the ball

Many players seem to believe that their job is done once they have passed the ball to a team-mate. However, when not in possession of the ball, a good attacking player is in continuous motion within the framework of the team's pattern of play. Individual attacking manoeuvres must be continuous and purposeful, and the attacker should try to initiate and direct moves with her passing. However, when not in possession of the ball, a good attacking player would be continuously 'thinking', moving and keeping the defender occupied. She will work to create space for her team-mates as well as back-up her attack and make herself available for a pass out of defence.

ATTACKING PLAY

Attack is easier than defence because the attacker knows when and where she is going, while the defender has to use intelligence and determination to overcome this 'think lag'. (For attacking tactics, see ch. 11.)

The most important aspects of attacking play are:
1 Timing.
2 Footwork.
3 Speed of reaction.

Timing

Timing is something that is very difficult to coach. Until a player can select the correct time to move into attack, she will not find it easy to make a positive contribution to the attacking moves of her team. The main problem with attackers are that they tend to move too soon (i.e. before their team-mate is ready to throw the ball) and therefore they are usually well-covered by a defending player by the time the ball is released; thus making the defence's job an easy one.

Task one: 'Go', or when to move

Two players with one ball. The players are free to move when and where they like, but the receiver must not start her move until the thrower shouts *'Go'*. The player with the ball must not give the signal until she is ready to throw (i.e. on balance and prepared).

The receiver should be coached to listen for the signal but, of paramount importance, *be looking for the visual cues* related to the signal. In this way an association will be formed between the visual display related to the throwing action and the attacking movement to *'Go'* and receive the ball.

Coaching points
The reliance on a verbal signal must not be continued for too long and as soon as possible the above skill must be repeated without a call—thus making the receiver decide *when* the correct time is to move.

This skill can be developed so that four players are used—moving to receive the ball in a given succession. At this stage, a further level of difficulty can be added, i.e. *moving off the ball*. The players are given a restricted area in which to move and receive a pass in turn. In this situation they should be moving continually so that they are adjusting their position relative to the player from whom they are to receive a pass. The *main* coaching point of this skill is that they show a clear change of speed between:

1 Manoeuvring for position,
2 Moving to receive the ball.

The latter should be done at optimum speed. In attacking play this is usually at the maximum speed the player can handle with control. Once the player has distributed the ball, she must be encouraged to *move off* the spot and reposition herself in readiness for the next pass—if she is needed.

Task Two: Timing with opposition
Three players (1 Feeder, 1 Defender, 1 Attacker) with one ball.

The Feeder with the ball starts with her back to the other two players, throws the ball in the air, catches it, and pivots round to face them.

The attacker must watch the feeder and decide when to move for the pass. The defender must be aware of the thrower and try to intercept the pass.

The three players continue in rotation and, out of five passes each, the attacker scores one point each time she catches the ball.

FOOTWORK AND SPEED OF REACTION

Attacking skills in netball are based on the ability to adjust:
— time.
— space.
— direction.
and use these to create a state of unbalance for the defence. Once the players know *when* to move they must then be taught *how* to evade the defence. All of these activities require the knowledge of *when* to go, vis. timing and the ability to move with agile and speedy footwork.

CHANGE OF SPEED—ANALYSIS OF THE SKILL

The straight sprint

A centre pass is the one time in the game when the straight sprint can be used to great effect. In this situation two opposing players, e.g. Wing Attack and Wing Defence, are presented with a territorial boundary which they cannot break until the whistle signal to start play is given.

Because of the line marking the off-side area, the Wing Attack is in position to screen off the space into which she will move by placing herself up to the line, and by using her feet to keep the Wing Defence behind her (see Fig. 9, ch. 5).

Coaching points

A narrow base is needed for mobility and both feet must be pointing in the direction in which the player is going to move. Weight is over the front foot—leaning forward—and knees are flexed, with sufficient muscular tension in the legs, thighs and hips to retain body balance. The back foot (i.e. the one nearest the opponent) must be up to the line to prevent her encroaching on the Attacker's space. On the whistle, the Attacker sprints out to receive the ball. A good starting position for this move is half-way along the third line. In this way the player is able to:

1 Move her feet in either direction, and counter a Defence repositioning to block her exit.

2 She has space to collect the ball without going too near the side-line.

3 By using a narrow angle of pathway out (this will depend on the position of the defending centre) she can take the ball near the third-line and thus will not have moved too far away from her own goal.

N.B. A player would not attempt this move if she is double-blocked by the opposing centre. She would also require her Goal Attack to 'lie back' off the line to (1) give the WA enough room to generate speed, (2) to be ready in the attacking third to receive a pass. A criticism of this move is that it is too easy to read. However, a fast Wing Attack in a 1-v-1 situation should be able to outrun her defence every time. In this case, *knowing* is not sufficient. The Wing Defence has to be able to stop her. This is usually done with help from another player, thus leaving another attacker free of an opponent. Therefore, in the main, this move is advantageous in that it is:

1 Very simple.

2 If done well, it can be very effective.

3 If double-blocked it can provide a decoy in that it uses two defenders to prevent it.

However, the straight sprint is not always the answer, and the player may have to use it in conjunction with some other move.

Sprint—stop—sprint

This is the type of move made by an attacker as the ball is being brought down the court, and where she has created large amounts of space for herself.

The player sprints fast in a given direction and then either completely stops, or decelerates to a jog, and then sprints again into the free space.

This play is used when an attacker finds that her defender is as quick as she is. The decelerating stop should catch the defender unawares, so that she too slows down and checks her forward movement; hopefully only to find the attacker sprinting off again in the same direction.

Sprint—change direction—sprint
In this case the attacker checks her forward speed and, pushing off from her leading foot, returns along the direction in which she has just travelled; hopefully leaving the defender to travel on alone and freeing her to receive a pass.

Developing the straight sprint

The development of the straight sprint is done in a way very similar to the way initiating motion was taught (see p. 26). The other two methods are taught quite simply by working in twos without a ball: The attacker working on one side of a line, the defender on the other. The attacker sprints, checks (or stops), and then sprints on along the line. The defender attempts to stay with her.

The same can be done with the change of direction, only this time the attacker returns along the pathway she has just followed. The use of the line helps to keep the players from cutting-off on diagonals.

The ball may be introduced into a group of three, i.e. a feeder and two workers, or it may be done as a group skill and used as a warm-up (see Fig. 30.)

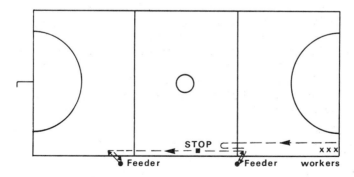

Fig. 30

Task
The players travel down the court and receives passes from the two feeders. The attack has only two ways to get free from her defence.

    1 Go—stop—go on

or

    2 Go—stop—go back.

The player has to decide which to use. If she gets the pass, she then stops, obeying the foot rule, adjusts her base, and passes back to the feeder, and moves on to the next feed.

CHANGE OF DIRECTION

The feint dodge

Where a player has a restricted area in which to move, and is closely marked, she has neither the time, or space, to use a sprint, and in this case she may find the feint dodge her best method of losing a defence.

Analysis of skill

A narrow base is needed, with the weight evenly distributed and taken over the balls of the feet. The knees should be flexed so that the body is in a position ready to move (the player may move on the spot, but beware of them simply bouncing up and down) and the trunk upright. The arms should be either straight at the sides, or with elbows bent and the hands at chest level ('Tommy Cooper' position—see Fig. 31).

    The essence of this dodge is the smallness of the cue to which the defence can respond. What the attacker should be trying to do is to feint to move in one direction but, in actuality, move in the other. If the attacker does too gross a movement in the decoy direction, she will be wasting time in that it will take her longer to recover from that position. This time is *defence time* and the slowness will allow the defence to recover her equilibrium. Therefore, what the attacker must try to do is to send the defence one way,

Fig. 31

while she moves in the other—without wasting time. This can be done by such gestures as:

1 A head nod.

2 A shoulder shake.

These *must* be *quick* and *decisive;* the defence has to think that the attacker is going that way.

At the same time as the decoy movement, the attacker should push-off from the foot furthest from the direction in which she is to move, and indicate clearly for the ball to be thrown into the space ahead of her hand. For example, the attacker nods her head deliberately to the *left* at the same time as she pushes-off from the *left* foot and moves away to the *right* to catch the ball.

Developing the skill

To develop the skill of the feint dodge, the following tasks are recommended:

Task One

Two players (1 attacker, 1 defender) but *no* ball. The players position themselves central of two parallel lines 3′ apart (see Fig. 32).

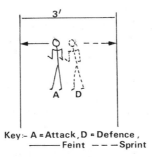

Key:- A = Attack, D = Defence,
——— Feint — — —Sprint

Fig. 32

The attacker has to try and lose her opponent by means of a feint dodge and be the first to reach one of the lines (i.e. if she feints right, it is the left line). The defender has to try and stay with her.

Coaching points

Players' bases should be narrow with weight on the balls of the feet—if necessary move 'on toes'. Balance is equal and knees are flexed. Players should try to use the smallest decoy to feint. Once the decision is made, they push from the far foot and, turning the body, sprint over the line.

Task Two

Three players with one ball.

Feeder starts with her back to players. She throws and catches the ball, turns and feeds the attacker, who feints one way and indicates to her free side.

Coaching points

Feeder: As soon as they see the feint, they must pass to the other side. They must not wait because to do so would give the defender time to adjust her position.

Attacker: They must get free sideways (i.e. they cannot ask for the ball over the top) and in a confined space. As soon as the feint occurs, they indicate to the free side and move quickly for the ball. Score out of five attempts:

  1 Number of successful dodges.
  2 Number of successful passes.
  3 Number of interceptions.
  4 Number of times ball is held.

The double dodge

If this type of play is used, it is essential that the thrower knows, otherwise she will have distributed the ball before the receiver has completed her feinting action.

In the double dodge the player can, for example do two feints:

Feint 1: Head gestures or shoulder dip to left.
Feint 2: Rock to right, push from right foot.
True move: Sprint left.

In the above, more time is taken because the second feint requires the weight to be momentarily transferred to the right before moving left. However, if well done, it is an extremely effective means of attack.

Pressure training

The most effective way to improve the dodge is by:

  1 Decreasing the space in which players have to get free.
  2 Increasing the opposition.

A valuable way to use pressure training is to make both shooters, with their defences, remain in the circle, and have 2 feeders outside the circle (Centre and Wing Attack) feed in a continuous flow of balls. The shooters, in a confined space closely marked by the defence (man-to-man marking), will find this a useful form of attack. They should be able to feint to both sides equally well because a defender will soon realise if an attacker always feints one way. Also, they may ideally make their final move towards the post, but this will depend on where in the circle they find themselves when they come to make their dodge.

To increase the pressure on centre court players, a 2-v-3 situation can be structured, using only the attacking one-third outside the circle. Here, players have more space than in the circle. However, they also have more opposition to contend with, as well as an asymmetric shape of court to cover. The scoring system for this could be 1 point every time the ball is caught following a dodge. For the defence—every time an interception is made.

The feint dodge need not only be made in a lateral plane, it can also be made front to back. The problem here can be that as the attacker feints forwards, she contacts the defender who is ahead of her. However, providing she has been given the space, a feint forwards and sideways, followed by a movement backwards away from the defender, can be very effective.

SPEED OF REACTION

Speed of responding to cues is essential for efficient attacking play, and 'reaction time' practices are by their very nature a good form of pressure training.

Task One
Two players, with one ball, facing each other with just slightly more than arm stretch between them.

The ball is passed, as quickly as possible, between the two. If they cannot catch, they volley or tap it back to their partner. The ball is passed:

1 Straight,
2 High,
3 Dropped,
4 Right/left.

Task Two
As above, but the space between is just slightly greater. One player has the ball, the other turns her back.

The ball is put into play, high, bounced, rolled, etc, and the player (whose back is turned) has to turn and collect the ball as quickly as possible.

Task Three
Two players; one with the ball and one sitting and facing her.

Player with ball tosses it into the air and sits down. The other player springs up and catches it before it touches the ground. When in her possession, she tosses it into the air and sits down.

Task Four
In two's as for Task 3; one Feeder, one Worker.

The feeder dictates how the worker starts, e.g. kneeling, lying on back. The feeder puts the ball into play, and the worker has to get up and catch it as quickly as possible (see Fig. 33 A,B,C).

Task Five
Three players, one feeder, two workers, with one ball. Players are positioned as shown in Figure 34 A and B.

Feeder with ball:

1 Dictates how the two workers start, e.g. sitting facing her behind the line.

A

B

C

Fig. 33A—C

2 On the command to play the two workers spring up, sprint to line, touch the ground and return to the feeder.

3 As they touch the ground, the feeder puts the ball into play, e.g. bounce, toss, roll, etc., and the quickest player back to the line gains possession.

To develop this task, the successful player may make a return pass to the feeder; this pass is defended (from 3′) by her opponent.

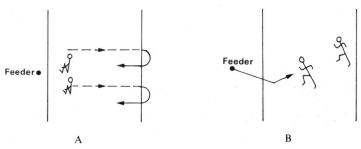

Fig. 34A—B

Task Six

Repeat task five but add a further variable by getting the feeder call 'right or left', as well as telling the player how to start.

The above tasks are not only of use to increase the players speed of reaction, but they are also fun and can help relieve the mental and physical fatigue that a hard training session can bring.

10
Defence

As mentioned in the previous chapter, defence may be considered as an individual or team skill. Good defence players can concentrate intensely, and are therefore able to react quickly to the visual clues they receive. Concentration is not a phenomenon, nor is it innate. It can be improved by devoting much time and effort to its achievement. The defender must be attack-minded so that she takes the initiative and constantly changes her tactics. The pressure she places on her opponent should be continuous and without relaxation. This way the attacker will be denied the opportunity of 'calling the tune'.

DEFENDING SKILLS

It is vitally important that every defender works to achieve certain fundamental skills. There are three important fundamentals to be considered in all defending manoeuvres, namely:

1 Footwork.
2 Body position.
3 Concentration, or attitude (mental).

Footwork

Footwork is very important and the defensive player must continuously alter her stance according to the immediate situation. She should also take up different positions as she adopts various strategies, i.e. marking or blocking the player, defending the pass or shot. The defender's weight should be evenly distributed on both feet, thus facilitating movement in any direction.

Body position

This is also important and, as far as possible when marking a player, the trunk should be held erect. This enables the defender to move quickly in any given direction. When marking the ball, it is essential that the defender leans to cover the ball without losing her balance and, therefore, the initiative.

Concentration/mental attitude

Concentration is essential, but when playing defence in a competitive situation it is sometimes more a matter of attitude and desire than the execution of specific skills. The defender's main task is to prevent the attacker receiving the ball. If she fails, it is essential that she does not lose her concentration, but immediately attempts to stop the pass, or shot. The ability to transfer quickly from defending a player to defending the ball is a skill which must be learnt and achieved at all levels.

MARKING A MOVING PLAYER

This type of play should be considered an essential skill for players, whatever their level of ability. It is extremely important that all players, attackers as well as defenders, are able to stay close enough to their opponents to intercept the pass, or force an error by the thrower or receiver. Once again, determination is a crucial element and if this can be combined with skill it will produce a successful defender. With beginners, the biggest problem is having to split their attention between the ball and opponent without losing sight of one or the other, or (even worse) both! The skill needs to be carefully built up and it is important that the defender experiences the joy of interception as early as possible.

Developing the skill

Task One: Follow the leader
The coach faces the players, who are spaced out in front of her. The players respond to movements or signals to send them to the left, right, forwards and backwards, keeping the movements short and sharp.

Working in 2's, travelling all over the court one behind the other, the leader changes her action (running, hopping, jumping) or speed, and is copied by her partner.

Working in 2's, or 3's, moving from one end of the court to the other, one player continually changes pace with her partner(s) attempting to match her speed.

Coaching points
Players need concentration and alertness so as to respond accurately to the cues given by teacher, coach, or partner. Feet should be kept under control by using small, rapid steps rather than 'giant' strides. Body position should be upright with weight over base so that change of direction or speed can be executed quickly.

Anticipation: By players closely watching the coach or partner it should be possible for them to read early cues and anticipate the next move.

Task Two

In 3's with one thrower, one receiver (dodger) and one marker. Initially restrict the dodger's movement to sideways only. This may be done by confining her between two parallel lines drawn on the court (see Fig. 35.)

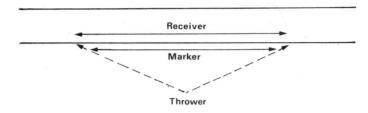

Fig. 35

Thrower calls the direction (left or right) that the receiver should move to catch the ball. This task can be developed by the receiver moving left or right, as she wishes.

Coaching points
The marker should hold her body upright and stand in front of the receiver. She should then place herself so that she covers half or three-quarters of her opponent's body with her own, *but* remains facing the ball.

The base should be narrow, and movement rapid, with small steps. Arms should not be dangling by the defender's side, but held with elbows bent in front of the chest—'Tommy Cooper' stance (see Fig 31, ch. 9.)

The beginner may often lose her opponent by turning to look for the ball too early. Initially, therefore, make them watch the opponent very carefully, only turning to look for the ball at the last possible moment. As players become more skilful, they will learn to split their attention between the opponent and the ball.

When the opponent moves out of vision behind the defender, this can often cause problems because the defender may turn her head too slowly. While she turns her head, the attacker may make another change of direction and be free. The defender must therefore learn to turn her head rapidly from side-to-side so that she keeps her opponent almost continuously in view.

If the defender is concentrating on her opponent she will need to know when the ball is coming. For beginners, the best cue is the movement of the attacker's arms that must move in order to receive the ball. As players become more skilful, they will learn to analyse their opponent's movements; by assessing a player's 'favourite' dodge, or 'strongest' catching side, it becomes easier to anticipate when and where the pass will arrive.

Task Three
In 4's, working in a confined area playing a game of 2-v-2.

Each couple is given ten passes. The defenders score one point if they touch or tip the ball, and two points if they intercept the ball and gain possession. The winning couple is the one who scores the most points.

A continuous game of 2-v-2; the attackers score a goal if they achieve seven successful consecutive passes, but the other team win possession every time they manage to touch, tip or intercept the ball.

Coaching points
The coaching points are the same as for task two, but with an added emphasis on persistance and team work.

Task Four
In 5's, working with one feeder (Centre) and two couples (Wing Attack/ Wing Defence; Goal Attack/Goal Defence).

The couples may be called A and B, with one attacker and one defender in each couple. The feeder (Centre) calls A or B, and the attacker must move to receive the pass. If the defender touches, tips or intercepts the pass, she then becomes the attacker.

Feeder stands in centre circle, couple A and B stand behind the third line. Centre calls 'play' and either attacker can move into the centre third to receive the pass.

Coaching points
As for task one and two, but with one notable exception where the defender is no longer in front of her opponent, but to one side. The defender must be well-balanced and ready to move explosively. Quite often the direction that the attacker will move is evident from the position she adopts on the line, and therefore the defender can move off immediately. However, the defender can also take some of the initiative away from the attacker by not allowing her to 'settle'. By moving intelligently from side-to-side, the defender may be able to force the attacker into a more difficult manoeuvre or cause the centre to make a poor pass.

MARKING A STATIC PLAYER

The word 'static' is perhaps misleading because few players are absolutely stationary when they receive the ball. However, there are different techniques required for marking a player who is simply 'holding her space'. Everyone has seen the *Queen Bee* (goal-shooter) who stands in the circle throughout the game just waiting to be fed with the ball by the workers who are busy outside the shooting circle. If the workers perform efficiently, the defence player will appear to have little or no chance of success. However, despite all the odds, there are certain things that the GK can do to improve her chances. She may vary her position in relation to her opponent in several ways:

1 *Standing in front* of the attacker. Many beginners, and younger players, should stand in front of their opponents and mark as described earlier. This type of marking may also be used by more advanced players while they attempt to assess their opponents' strengths and weaknesses. If they find that they are achieving success this way there will be no need to look further.

2 *Standing behind* an opponent. This allows the defender to watch her opponent and see the ball coming down the court. This obviously has

advantages as it is possible for the GK to see the ball early and move out to intercept. However, it requires great speed and agility to manoeuvre around the shooter without causing contact. The disadvantages are also obvious, as an intelligent attacking team will work the ball close to the circle and then make a short, sharp pass into the space in front of the shooter. There is also a tendency for the defender to make contact with her arms or body as she attempts to intercept or deflect the ball.

3 *Standing at right angles.* This is when the defender takes up a position at the side of the attacker, either facing her, or with her back towards her; forming a right angle between her own body and the body of her opponent If possible the defender should position herself so that the attacker has to move *away* from the feeder, and consequently forces a long pass which may be intercepted. For example, if the ball is being passed down the left-hand side of the court, the defender stands on the same side of her opponent so that the shooter is prevented from moving towards the ball. The pass she receives will therefore be long and high, giving the defender an opportunity to move quickly alongside the shooter and intercept.

Every defender should experiment with all three types of stance to determine their own most successful method. However, it is also essential that they are able to adapt to any of the three stances so as to obtain greater versatility and the ability to vary tactics.

BLOCKING

This is a method of defending where the defender prevents her opponent from moving into a desired area. Blocking can be most frequently seen when used by the Goal Defence working to stop the Goal Attack getting into the shooting circle. This is simply *one* of the defender's many skills and should not be her only ploy.

Too often a defender forsakes the ball completely in an attempt to block out her opponent. This may be justified in certain situations, but in most cases it needs to be combined with other modes of defence.

Developing the skill

Task One
Working in 3's in a confined area. Two players (B and C) stand one behind the other in a channel marked by two parallel lines. The third player (A) faces them and then attempts to manoeuvre around them remaining in the channel and avoiding contact (see Fig. 36).

Players B and C practise their blocking techniques.

Coaching points
Players should have a small base with weight evenly distributed over both feet to facilitate quick changes of direction. They should also use rapid small steps to move from side-to-side. The body should be upright, with the

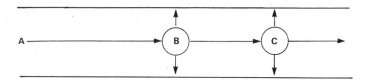

Fig. 36

shoulders square to the oncoming player—the shoulders do *not* turn. Arms must be kept at side.

Task Two
In 3's with a ball. Player A starts with the ball and Player B defends the pass to Player C and then tries to block Player A from moving down the channel to receive the return pass (see Fig. 37).

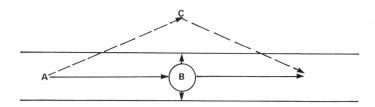

Fig. 37

Player B defends the pass and then blocks.

Coaching points
The blocker must keep her feet on the ground when defending a pass. A common fault is that the defender jumps to intercept a pass and her opponent goes round her while she is still in the air. The blocker must be able to quickly adjust from leaning forward to cover the pass, to the upright blocking stance. They *must* concentrate on watching the opponent and not be distracted by the pass. Once the blocker has been passed, she must turn quickly, and attempt to mark her opponent and prevent her receiving the return pass.

Task Three
4-v-4 on court: Centre (C), Wing Attack (WA), Goal Attack (GA), Goal Shooter (GS), *vs* Centre, Wing Defence (WD), Goal Defence (GD), Goal-Keeper (GK).

Starting at the centre, players pass with the condition that those who fail to intercept must defend the pass and then block their opponent. Play is continuous until a goal is scored, or the defence gain possession, and work the ball past the centre of the court.

Coaching points

The defenders must not lunge through for wild interceptions. (They will not get the ball, or be able to block their opponent effectively.) Rapid change is needed from blocking to marking in front of the opponent. Begin to highlight the most effective times and places to use blocking, e.g. circle edge. If the blocking is to be successful it is essential that the blocker gets up close to her opponent, allowing her as little room to manoeuvre as possible.

Blocking in the full game

This is not a method of defence which should be over-encouraged with beginners, or youngsters, but it cannot be neglected or ignored. There are obviously some specific cases, and places, where blocking can be a very effective tactic. One example has already been given on p. 78 where a Goal Defence uses it to prevent the Goal Attack getting into the circle. It may also be used to break-up an opposition's rhythms in the centre of the court. For example, many Centres are familiar with passing the ball and then immediately moving off to receive the return. However, if they are blocked, this prevents them moving quickly forward and subsequently breaks up the attacking pattern.

DEFENDING THE PASS

Once the attacker has out-witted the defence, and has possession of the ball, the defender must concentrate on preventing the next pass. The rules determine that the defender must be at least 3' away from the attacker's landing foot, or feet. She has two alternative methods of attempting to intercept the pass. She may either jump to intercept, or simply keep both feet firmly on the ground while using her reach and arm length to guard the ball.

Developing the skill

Task One

In 2's with a ball. One player stands about 10' from a target, or marker, on a wall or fence. She throws the ball several times, while the second player observes. Then the second player takes up a position 3' in front of the thrower and attempts to intercept the throw by:

    1 Keeping feet on the ground,
    2 Jumping to intercept.

Coaching points

Players should observe an opponent's style of passing, looking specifically at the moment of release. Both feet should be kept on the ground and the ball guarded by hand(s) being placed over the ball. The ball's path should be followed, wherever the opponent moves it while preparing to throw.

Arms need to be bent, in front of chest, and knees slightly flexed waiting to spring to intercept. Opponents must be closely watched so as to anticipate moment of release.

Task Two

In 3's with one thrower, one dodger, and one marker. The defender marks her opponent and, if she fails to intercept, she turns to mark the ball. Initially, with beginners, it may be necessary to make the thrower wait before returning the ball, otherwise the defender gets little chance to defend the pass. With more advanced players this can become a continuous and exhausting practice.

Coaching points

Players need to achieve rapid change from defending a player to defending a pass, and vice versa. They must also be alert, ready to move and use rapid, small steps to cover the necessary ground. Lunging through for the interception must be avoided as this makes it difficult to get back to defend the pass.

Task Three

In 4's: 2-v-2 game in a confined area. Place a condition on the game so that the thrower waits 3 seconds between receiving and passing the ball. This helps the defender to guard the ball, as well as mark the player. The defending team win possession every time they touch, tip, or intercept any pass.

Defending the pass in the game

The coach needs to help the players assess the relative advantages, or disadvantages, of the two methods of interception in the game. There are clear cases where one method is preferable to the other, but generally the player needs to *think* for herself. The relative heights of the two players concerned is obviously a consideration, plus the position on the court. For example a centre, with an opponent of the same height, may find it beneficial to jump to intercept a pass into the shooting circle, but find it better to keep both feet on the ground in the centre court. This would enable her to move off quickly in pursuit of her opponent if she fails to make an interception. Other examples may be found at opposite ends of the court where a Goal Shooter may choose to jump to attempt to intercept the Goal-Keeper's back line pass, whereas Goal Defence will almost definitely keep her feet on the ground when defending the Goal Attack's pass as she will probably block her after the ball has gone.

DEFENDING THE SHOT

This is a very important skill for every Goal Defence and Goal-Keeper to acquire. As with defending the ball in court, there are two clear options.

Either they can (1) jump to attempt to intercept, or (2) simply keep both feet on the ground and cover the shooters movements with their hand(s).

The aim of their action is to deflect or intercept the shot, or to cause the shooter to alter her usual shooting technique, and therefore possibly score fewer goals. It may be advisable to use both methods in the same game as this change of tactics can unsettle the shooter. However, there are also other factors to be considered:

1 The relative heights of the two players. For example, a tall Goal Keeper marking a smaller Goal Shooter may be able to disrupt her action by simply stretching out and covering the ball with her hand(s); whereas a small Goal Defence may decide it is better to jump to intercept the taller Goal Attacks shot as she has insufficient reach to cause problems the other way.

2 The shooter's style may also determine the defence's decision. If the shooter has a low action, it may be easier for the defender to stretch and cover the ball, thus forcing her to change her natural shooting action. Alternatively, a shot from a player who uses a high action may successfully be intercepted by jumping.

Developing the skill

Task One
Players experiment individually to determine the best stance to get the longest possible reach. Players should stand away from the netting around the court (or something similar) and try to touch the netting first with a jump, and then with both feet on the ground.

Coaching points
A sideways stance should be adopted as this enables a longer reach than standing square. Everyone will have a 'favourite' side, but encourage all players to try both sides—they may surprise themselves! Slight flexion of the knees will achieve a greater spring. Discourage a big preparation, as it is unlikely in the game that the defender will have time to use a deep knee bend. When standing, the player can lean (*under control*) to see if she can touch the netting (3' away).

Task Two
In 2's with a ball. One player shoots using various techniques, and the defender selects the appropriate action—see factors 1 and 2 above.

Coaching points
Individual assistance should be given to players to help them assess a situation and take the appropriate action. Whatever action is taken, it must be sustained for 3 seconds, or until the shooter has taken her shot.

Players should jump towards the shooter so that they intercept the flight of the ball. The arm should be outstretched towards the ball, not waving aimlessly in front of the face, 'cleaning windows'! Having jumped, the defender must drop her arm and retreat 3' before taking a second jump.

Players must also lean-in towards the shooter, with arm outstretched and hand over the ball. Over-balancing should be avoided as this brings the defender within 3' of the shooter and therefore breaks the rules.

Task Three
In 3's, with one feeder, one shooter and one defender. The defender marks the shooter, who is fed from outside the circle. If the defender fails to intercept the pass then she must immediately defend the shot.

Coaching points
The defender must not lunge through for wild interceptions, allowing the shooter a 'free' shot at goal. She should also concentrate on marking the attacker closely before turning rapidly to defend the shot, but ensure she is 3' from the shooter before lifting her arms. If the defender fails to intercept the shot she must endeavour to retrieve the rebound.

Task Four
In 8's with Centre, Wing Attack, Goal Attack, Goal Shooter *vs* Centre, Wing Defence, Goal Defence, Goal-Keeper (half-court game.)
Playing from the centre, the ball is passed towards the shooter. Goal-Keeper and Goal Defence work against their opponent, but adjust their action according to the situation.

Coaching points
The defender needs to consider her action once the ball has left the shooter's hand. The two defenders should discuss their tactics (see ch. 11) and respond accordingly. For example, if the defender has decided to block the shooter after the shot to prevent her following in, then she should *not* jump to intercept the shot; thus allowing her fellow defender a chance to collect the rebound.

11
Tactics

The previous chapters have dealt with individual skills and the necessity for each player to achieve proficiency in those skills that will equip her for the role she is to play in a game. The game, however, involves much more than skills. It includes the flexible use of skill to deal with ever-changing situations. This presents the coach with her most difficult and important task. Namely, the blending of the skills of her team into effective 'in-game' tactics.

Netball is a very simple game. From school to international level, the tactics are very similar. The only real difference is in the ability to apply these tactics. It is the speed and precision of internationals that marks their play, not the tactics they employ.

Unfortunately, because of the rule-dictated structures of the game, netball has become very stereotyped. It is almost as if flair and individuality have been coached out of the game. The unexpected and the unorthodox are the most difficult moves for any opponent to counter. The player whose responses are highly individual (always given that this individuality is successful) can be a match winner in that her opponent, or even opponents, are so busy trying to assess what she will do next, that they can almost be discounted as part of their team defence. This type of flair for the game is *not* coachable, but what the coach must try to do is harness this ability to the advantage of her own team.

Unfortunately this type of player can create as many problems for her own team as for the opposition. She will see situations arising far in advance of other players on the team. Her anticipation, speed of movement, or pass, may be such that her own team-mates are unable to cope. This can lead not only to a breakdown in play, but also friction between players both on and off the court. The role of the coach here is to attempt to develop a sympathetic union between her players so that the most efficient compromise possible is reached.

Netball is an open skill, i.e. the spatial and temporal environment is not fixed. Players move, the ball is passed, defences pose different problems for attacks. This means that whatever tactics are coached the players should understand that they are only the basic plans. These plans must be capable of in-game modification and adaption according to what is currently happening on the court. When coaching tactics to players who are mature and skilful, the coach should make it plain that they alone must select the most appropriate action to deal with the opposition. This is not to say that the coach should abdicate all responsibility for what happens on court. On the contrary, this is a very important aspect of her role. So often it is easier to see what is happening from off the court than when actually playing.

Therefore, the coach is responsible for laying the plans, and using her observation of the game to guide her team in selecting the most appropriate tactic to deal with the current situation.

ATTACKING TACTICS

With any tactic in any game, a player should adopt the following general principle:

Do not change a winning tactic, and always change one which is failing.

It is a very disturbing fact that, even at the highest level, players continue to repeat the same tactical move even when it is obvious that it is failing. It is true that each individual has a style and method of play which they perform better than anything else, but in an open skill this will, unfortunately, not always be the most successful method, therefore this method must be varied and adapted until a correct answer is found. This process of analysis and evaluation must be made as quickly as possible. There is little point in a player deciding in the last five minutes of a match that trying to out-run her opponent was the incorrect answer, especially when her team are losing, and she has received so few passes that they have in fact only been playing with six!

Achieving continuity of attack

Anyone who watched the Australian 1978/1979 touring side could only have been too aware of the importance of *continuity of attack*. This continuity in attack may be achieved if players are made aware how important the following factors can be to their play.

Anticipation

Anticipation could be described as the ability to make a judgement about future moves based on information from present play. Each player should attempt to 'read' the game at least two moves ahead of her own position, and two moves behind her. To do this she must *assess:*

1 The space available on her own side and the oppositions.

2 The time available.

3 From whom she is most likely to receive a pass and where that pass will be made, and where the thrower's opponent will be when the ball is thrown.

4 To whom she will pass when she has secured the ball, and how the oppositions' positions may influence this decision.

These types of judgement can take a long time to become established, and it is only by continuously highlighting the relevant cues that players will eventually be able to function independently.

Another vitally important aspect of anticipation is that all players need to be aware of exactly what is happening throughout the *whole game.* In this way they can ensure that they are ready to react to *any* situation which may arise, no matter how unexpected or unorthodox.

Timing the move

The timing of the attacking move is again very important, but is unfortunately very difficult to coach. For example:

1 If a player moves too soon, she would allow her defender to position herself so as to make the reception of a pass impossible.

2 If a player moves too late, the attacking continuity would break down, or she would be omitted from the sequenced play.

The timing of the move is based on judging when the thrower is going to release the ball. This will vary with each individual, in each particular set of circumstances. It is by exposing players to a variety of such situations that the coach assists them to develop their own decision-making processes. However, in the final analysis, only the player can make such decisions and often this remains the 'achilles heel' of many players throughout their whole playing career.

Surprise

The value of a surprise attack has always been admitted in military terms, and the same holds good on the games field. For instance:

1 Players should be coached not to continuously use the same speed, rhythm and spatial pathway. It is far too simple for a defender to decode. As with other aspects of the game, the player should be encouraged and assisted to develop a skill repertoire which will afford her a wide selection of options.

2 Players should be coached to be aware of the 'surprise' moves their own side may make. There is little value to be gained if a surprise move catches their team unaware and leads to a breakdown and loss of the ball.

N.B. It must again be repeated that if the tactic being played is successful *do not change it*. Players are not on the court to demonstrate their versatility, but to use it, *as necessary,* to win the match. Players are frequently criticised for only doing one thing (e.g. running as opposed to dodging), but if she is being successful there should be no reason for change. This does not necessarily mean she cannot do anything else, but merely that at the time it is *not necessary* for her to do so.

Selection

Choice of the most appropriate method of attack will depend on the circumstances of play. They may be as follows:

1 Speed: if the space is available to accelerate.

2 Dodge: if confined by space and opposition.

3 Dodge and spring: if the opponent cannot be beaten by straight speed.

4 Block: the space to create a free channel for the ball to be placed.

This merely re-states that players must be *thinking* as well as *moving*.

Ambidexterity

Players should learn to move equally well to both sides of the body, and catch the ball with either hand. The asymmetric reach with one hand is greater than a symmetrical reach with two. Advanced players may be forced by the defence to take the ball at full stretch, and should therefore practise taking the ball on either hand while fully extended both upwards and sideways. However, it must be stressed that, for safety reasons, players should *get the other hand on the ball as fast as possible.*

Aerial space

If players have a good natural spring (and many netball players do) use this to its full. Work for ankle flexibility, leg strength and power to increase and enhance this ability. Players should also practise taking the ball high directly overhead, and to either side. To do this successfully, the team must be able to throw accurately to capitalise on this skill. A badly placed ball, which is neither high or wide, will only succeed in reaching the defender. Players do need to develop the ability to take-off from either foot and be able to adjust base while in the air so that they are in the best position possible to release the ball immediately they land.

N.B. Other players in the team must remember that they must adjust their move for the ball based on *the time it takes for the receiver to land* and distribute the pass. The higher or wider a player travels, the longer she will take to adjust.

Breadth of attack

As a basic attacking tactic, a team should spread their attack as wide as possible. In this way they will make the defence cover the widest possible area. If an attacking team adopt this tactic they must ensure that, as the ball covers this space, it is passed with speed, directness and precision; ball in the air is a *defence ball.*

One way to achieve a breadth of attack on the full court is described in chapter 14. Around the attacking circle, the greatest spread would be achieved by having three players outside the circle, feeding one shooter. In this way the players 'pivot' around the player in the centre of the court and spread their attack to cover both corners and the middle (see Fig. 38A and B).

Players should not remain static in the positions shown in Figure 38, but 'give and go', switching and exchanging positions so that ball and players are moving at a speed to create a gap in defence that allows the shooter to be fed. If the two circle defences move onto the shooter to double-mark her, she should attempt to move away from the post. Goal Attack will immediately move into the circle (avoiding and defending centre court players who may be trying to keep her out) and adopt the role of shooter, receive the pass and make a shot.

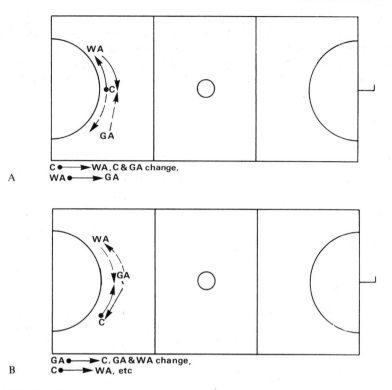

Fig. 38A—B

DEFENCE TACTICS

The main tactic for all defences is to prevent the opposition scoring a goal. This may be achieved in several quite different ways, or a combination of them all. The important basic principle is to use the method that most unsettles the opposition. Too often teams practise a particular system and then go to a match and play it, *despite* the opposition's tactics. It is far more sensible for players to be equipped with several alternatives, and use the most appropriate. To be able to do this they must be *thinking* and assessing the opposition as soon as the game begins. This involves each individual 'testing out' their opposite number: Does she always use a particular dodge? Does she prefer to catch with her right or left hand? Does she always receive a pass from the same player?

Once the defender has found the strengths and weaknesses of her opponent, she can then begin to create problems for them. As well as this individual assessment, there must also be an awareness of the overall attacking tactics of the other team: Are all the goals being scored by one particular shooter? Is the Goal Defence always used by the Goal-Keeper at back line passes? Is there a set pattern of play from the centre pass? It is not easy to see all these things while playing, but it is important that players are able to make these observations. This is also an area where a team coach may be of positive assistance during the game, although she too will find it difficult to focus her attention on the opposition instead of her own players 'performance'.

Man-to-man defence

Each player is responsible for marking one member of the opposite team. The defending skills (see p. 74) will obviously be used by each individual. The marking method selected will be determined by the relative strengths and weaknesses of the defender and attacker. These could include blocking, right-angle marking, marking in front, or marking from behind. It may be necessary to keep changing the technique to prevent the attacker from settling into a rhythm. It is essential to take the attacker's initiative away by dominating her.

There are also occasions where defenders will perhaps find it beneficial to *switch* players. The advantage of 'switching', as opposed to a formal change of position at half-time, is that a team's well-practised tactics will not be totally disrupted. A clear example of this may be seen in the shooting circle where the Goal Defence switches to mark the Goal Shooter and Goal-Keeper marks the Goal Attack. There are several reasons why this may be done:

1 *Relative heights* of the players involved (e.g. if the Goal Shooter is much taller than the Goal-Keeper, and is being fed easily by her own team). If the Goal Defence is taller than her team-mate, they may decide to change opponents as the ball is brought down towards the circle. This requires a good understanding between them, and excellent timing, as any misunderstanding will leave the attackers unmarked at a crucial time. This may be too difficult for younger players, but it is possible for them to use 'dead ball' situations, such as throw-ins, a throw-up, or centre passes, to bring about the change. (See ch. 13 and 14 for further analysis of these passes.)

2 'Switching' may also be necessary after a penalty has been awarded against a player. If the other player moves rapidly, it is occasionally possible to reduce the immediate dangers, particularly in the circle.

3 At a centre pass the attackers (Goal Attack and Wing Attack) may change sides at the last moment and the defenders switch players in order to mark more efficiently. This should not be encouraged, except in an emergency, because it can create problems when players try to switch back again.

4 In the circle, the Goal Attack and Goal Shooter may use each other as a shield to evade their defenders. In these 'tight' situations it may be easier for players to simply 'pick up' the nearest player rather than worry about chasing their positional opponent.

This flexibility of tactics, and the ability to change the stereotyped method of marking, often surprises the opposition to such an extent that they make a mistake and lose possession.

Zone defence

This is an effective method of defending if used for short periods in the game as a 'surprise' tactic, or in order to break the other team's rhythm. However, if used for too long, it is easily broken down by an intelligent attacking team. In zoning, each defender marks an area of the court rather than a particular player. The problem for most players when introduced to zoning for the first time is that they find it difficult to watch the ball rather than their opponent. This type of defence can be developed with the use of the following tasks.

Task One
Working in pairs with a ball, the defender stands in front of a goal area (marked on a wall, or court surround) and the other player throws the ball, in a controlled manner, trying to 'score a goal' by getting the ball past the defender.

Coaching points
The defender must be on her toes, bouncing gently, and ready to move in either direction.

The defender must catch the ball, pass back to the thrower who returns it rapidly to the centre of the defender's goal in her position of readiness.

The defender must concentrate on the ball and study the thrower's technique.

Task Two
Working in a group of four with a ball, one thrower, one defender, two 'posts'. The distance between the posts will vary according to the ability of the defender (Fig. 39).

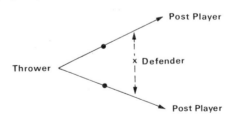

Fig. 39

The thrower (who may *not* move to receive the pass) may throw to either post and the defender attempts to intercept.

Coaching points
As for task one above, but with an important addition. The defender must *not* turn to see what the posts are doing, but concentrate on the thrower. This is an important principle to establish if zoning is to be successful later.

Task Three
In a group of six with a ball, 3 posts, 2 defenders, 1 thrower (see Fig. 40).

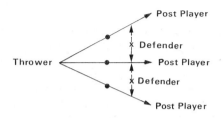

Fig. 40

The thrower may pass to any of the three posts. The defenders work together to intercept the ball.

Coaching points
As for tasks one and two above, but now the team-work becomes the vital factor.

Use the defenders' strengths. For example, if one player is more capable of catching on the left, then she should work on that side of the zone.

The middle play will be vulnerable unless team-work is practised. It is better for the strongest player to go for the interceptions and for the other player to cover her. To do this successfully, without a mid-air collision, means one player must stand slightly in front of the other (Fig. 41).

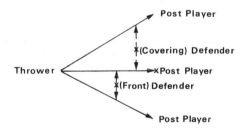

Fig. 41

Task Four
A group of seven with a ball. As shown for task three, but with an additional thrower. The two throwers pass the ball between themselves and, when they feel they have the defence out of position, they throw to one of the posts.

Coaching points
The defending pair must adjust their position according to the position of the ball so that they narrow the angle of the pass (Fig. 42).

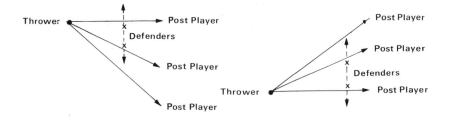

Fig. 42

ZONING IN THE GAME

Half court practice

Initially Goal Shooter only in the circle, Goal Attack and Wing Attack out wide near the side lines, Centre just inside the defending third line (Fig. 43).

Team Work is Vital. Centre and Wing Defence (working together) move around the circle edge keeping between the ball and the goal. Goal Defence and Goal-Keeper alter their positions in the circle depending on the location of the ball.

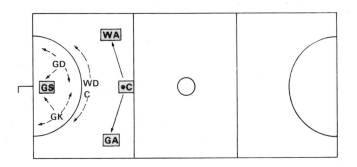

Fig. 43

Attackers (GA, C and WA) pass the ball round and attempt to feed the shooter while the defenders (C, WD, GD, GK) work to intercept the ball.

The movement of the attackers is unrestricted. Play is started by a centre pass and the defenders must immediately drop back into their zone positions.

Full team zone

This is formed when the opposition are taking a back line throw-in (Fig. 44).

Goal Shooter attempts to cut out pass in the end third. Goal Attack and Wing Attack zone side-by-side in the centre third.

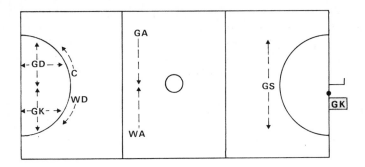

Fig. 44

Coaching points
It is essential that all players get into position rapidly. Goal Shooter, Goal
Attack and Wing Attack should attempt to intercept passes or block
players moving down court.

All players must move into position without turning their backs and
'running away' from the ball!

Once the zone is broken, i.e. a player is drawn out of position, the players
must *immediately return to man-to-man defence.*

SUMMARY

Coaches must remember that sound tactics are essential for an efficiently
operating team. Skills are essential in implementing tactics, but many
highly skilful players can have great difficulty in applying these skills in the
game. It is therefore important that whatever aspect is being coached, i.e.
skills or tactics, it be done in a realistic manner. If the skill or tactic does not
occur in netball, there is little point in practising it, except perhaps as a
form of pressure training. It is stressed here that realism should be in the
form of:

1 The correct space or direction.

2 The correct time.

3 At some stage, against the correct opposition.

By simulating realistic situations, the coach is preparing her players to
be able to reproduce their skills and tactics when it counts. Namely, in the
competitive match situation.

12
Warm Up

The warming-up of a team is important because its use with a well-organised team, or individual, can be the first weapon in a coach's armoury. The team which is out warming-up 15–20 minutes pre-match, going through a well thought-out routine, is a team which takes the game seriously. To the opposition, before they have taken to the court of play, this can be a source of stress, particularly if their own warm-up only consists of jogging a couple of laps of the court with every player following and, irrespective of their position, shooting for goal. To the team, an efficient warm-up can act as a psychological prop. Many players do become anxious pre-match and giving them something constructive and relatively vigorous to perform will help them concentrate on the task in hand; rather than spending the time building-up tension and wasting energy by worrying about what is to follow.

PHYSIOLOGICAL ASPECTS

In addition to any psychological benefits the warm up may impart, there are also sound physiological reasons why a team should *not* walk directly onto the court and commence to play. It is not within the scope of this book to put forward an in-depth explanation of the physiology of exercise, but, making the case for the inclusion of the warm up in the preparation for competition, it is felt that the coach should at least have a 'nodding acquaintance' with some of the physiological reasons for its inclusion.

Background

In very simple terms, we are concerned with the mechanisms of the body which allow the player to perform physical work, i.e. to play. Basically, there are two systems:

    1 The energy transport system which is concerned with the carrying of food and oxygen from the environment to the cells, namely the cardiovascular system.

    2 The energy transfer system which is concerned with the transfer of energy (metabolism) from the food to the 'energy currency' of ATP which is used by the cells to perform work.

    It is not proposed to discuss the dietary intake or digestive processes involved; sufficient to know that we eat in order to provide the cells with the energy to do work. What will be outlined is the process involved in achieving this energy production:

1 Oxygen is an essential part of this process and is inhaled from the atmosphere to the lungs.

2 This oxygen is transported to the muscle cells in haemoglobin, or red cells of the arterial blood.

3 The heart acts as a pump; the oxygen carrying blood being pumped out of the left-side of the heart via the arteries, to the muscles.

4 At cellular level, energy transfer takes place and food is converted to energy and, as a result, waste products are produced.

5 The waste products are carried via the veins to the right-side of the heart, and from there to the lungs to be exhaled back into the atmosphere.

Physiological support

Expressed very simply, warm-up could be said to increase the body temperature. If this is so, then, as a consequence, the following should occur:

1 The metabolic rate (energy transfer), which is essential for the body to do work, *increases*. It is said that for each 1° increase in temperature the metabolic rate increases by 13%. Therefore, increasing the rate at which energy is produced affords the body a greater capacity to do work.

2 The heart rate increases and therefore the circulatory rate of the blood.

3 The respiratory capacity increases, resulting in more oxygen being available for transfer to the muscles.

So far only the mechanisms involved in doing work have been outlined. There is one very important body system which carries out this work. This is the muscular system and it is by muscular contraction that the body is able to move. The contraction of muscle is very much temperature dependent. If the temperature is low, muscle contractitility decreases with the concomitant decrease in its capacity to do work. Therefore, an increase in temperature makes contraction easier and hence increases the capacity to work. An increase in temperature can also decrease the viscosity or stickiness of the muscle, therefore serving to facilitate contraction. So, in purely physiological terms, warm-up can be seen to impart certain benefits to performance.

OTHER REASONS FOR WARM-UP

As well as physiological and psychological factors, other reasons are often put forward when arguing the case for warm-up. Two such arguments are:

1 The prevention of injury.

2 In general terms, as an aid to increased performance.

Prevention of injury

Unfortunately, there is little hard evidence to support the theory that warm-up prevents injury as normally there is extreme difficulty in proving if warm-up has actually taken place. Most athletes, even in an experimental situation, are extremely reluctant to commence vigorous exercise cold; and there appears to be some doubt about experimental evidence that has been produced on this basis. However, physiologically, the decrease in muscle viscosity should give a greater flexibility and therefore cut down the chance of injury due to muscle tear.

Muscle injuries tend to occur at two stages in the game:

1 Early with the implication that the player is not yet warm enough to operate safely.

2 In the later stages of the game when fatigue is usually the cause.

It must therefore be re-stated that while it is generally accepted that the warm-up *should* help to prevent muscle injury, there is little actual proof that it does so.

Increased performance

As with injury, there is also little evidence to support the hypothesis that warm-up improves performance; despite all the physiological advantages to be gained from it. However, research does indicate that the most positive effects can be gained from a general, non-specific warm-up, followed, where necessary, by a warm-up which is specific to the skill components of the event. It would appear that where the integration of complex skills are required for the actual game, the refamiliarisation with them pre-match should improve in-game performance. Netball is a game which involves endurance, speed and skill components and therefore the pre-match warm-up should be both specific and non-specific.

SPECIFIC WARM-UPS

Warm-ups for netball should include:

1 *Locomotor activities* (running, hopping, springing, bounding)
   Alone.
   In pairs.
   In groups.

These may be of a cooperative and competitive nature. For example, in a 1-v-1, or with 4 players, making a relay team to compete against another team.

2 *Flexibility exercises,* examples of which can be found in Mobility Exercises, P.R. Harper, BAAB Publications, 1971.

3 *Ball Skills.* These could be fun type activities, individual or group skills, or set pieces from the game (see ch. 13).

Examples of locomotor activities

The following activities can be employed when introducing warm-up:

1 Running round the court, jumping to touch various points marked around the court.

2 Jogging (using all the space). On the sound of the whistle, players sprint and, on the second blast, return to jogging. (Players alone, then against a partner.)

3 Running about the court. When the whistle blows, players jump and land using the correct footwork. (Running, jumping, landing and 'giving' to prevent travelling forward.)

4 Moving forwards, backwards, and left and right depending on the coach's direction, players working alone and then in cooperation with a partner; then in competition with an opponent.

5 Jumping up and down on the spot (two small jumps followed by right down and up on third jump.)

6 Running about the court. When the whistle blows, players jump, land with correct footwork, pivot and move off again. Working between two lines, they run and jump to land on the line, pivot, run back to the other line and repeat.

7 Running about the court. When the whistle blows, players change direction as quickly as possible.

8 In 2's, changing direction. The front player is the controller. Her partner is standing behind her. The front player then moves forwards, backwards and sideways, with the back player shadowing her movements.

9 One player puts a band, or tape, in the back of her shorts. Her partner must try to capture the tape and snatch it away. This should take place in a limited amount of space. Do not attempt this unless the children are sensible and mature enough to cope!!

10 Shuttle relays (using teams of 4 or 5), players run to touch a line and then back to the team. The next runner sets off as soon as the incoming player touches her.

11 Progressive relay. Players touch one line, run back, then return to touch second line, and so on, over a given distance. For example, the full court.

12 British Bulldog. One player 'A' stands in the middle of the court. The rest of the class stand on the base-line of the court. They must run to the other end, staying within the limits of the court. 'A' tries to touch as many players as possible. Once caught, the others join 'A' in the middle and help her 'trap' the rest of the class. (Continue until everyone is caught.)

Tag games
With many younger players, warm-up can take the form of tag games, such as those outlined below:

Partner tag
Working in pairs, players link arms and run. There are two 'free' runners, one being 'IT' and the other to be caught. The latter hooks onto any pair before 'IT' touches her below the waist. The individual at the other end of the now 'trio' becomes the runner to be caught. If this runner is caught, she becomes 'IT'.

Circle guard

Chalk a 4' diameter circle on the floor. A group of 5 or 6 pupils form a circle round the chalk-circle and hold hands. They try to pull a member of the group into the chalk-circle without breaking the grasp. If the circle is broken, reform and start again (see Fig. 45).

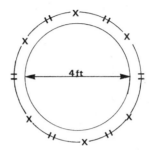

Fig. 45

Circle tag

Two players hold both arms (wrist grasp) and chase the other pupils, 'tagging' them with their free hands by touching them below the waist. The two players only release their grasp on each other to make contact. 'Tagged' players join the two chasing players, forming a larger circle.

Caterpillar tag

Two players chase the rest of the class and try to 'tag' them by touching them below the waist. If a pupil is 'tagged' she goes behind the player who 'tagged' her, grasping her round the wasit. The 'caterpillar' now chases the rest of the class. The two teams can compete to achieve the largest 'caterpillar'.

Colour drop tag

Four teams with different coloured braids. The coach calls a colour and the team with that colour chase the other teams. As the members of the other teams are touched below the waist, they skip-jump. The length of time taken to catch the others can be recorded.

French tag

A player (or players) chase the class and 'tags' another pupil from behind, below the wasit. The tagged pupil holds the part of the body that is 'tagged' with one hand and with the free hand tries to 'tag' another pupil.

Team tag

Four teams, each with different coloured braids. One team chases the rest of the class by hopping, and 'tags' the members of the other teams below the waist. If one of the chasing team members wants to change hopping legs, she must stop and perform three skip-jumps first. The length of time taken to catch the other teams can be recorded.

Lame dog tag

All pupils 'run' on all fours, except the 'tagger' (or 'taggers') who have to keep one leg off the ground. The pupils who are 'tagged' from the waist downwards, help the 'tagger' (or 'taggers').

Dodge and mark
Working players in pairs, numbering 1 and 2, the 2's chase the 1's on the word 'Go', but they must always try to remain within touching distance. On the whistle, 1's and 2's immediately stop. The 2's reach out to see whether or not they can touch 1's.

PRE-COMPETITION WARM-UP

Event tactics should start well before the whistle to commence play. Given that the coach knows what time the game is scheduled to start, the warm-up should commence approximately 25–30 minutes before that time in order to gain maximum benefit.
The following is a suggestion of a pre-match warm-up:

General phase

All players jog three laps of the court.
All players jog and sprint alternate thirds of the court.
The whole team work together on ball handling skills.

Skill: Phase One
Defence players (GK and GD) work together on a keeping goal practice (see p. 111.)
GS and GA practise shooting from different distances and angles. The three centre court players work on throw-ups.

Skill: Phase Two
GK and GD move into the circle and play against GS and GA. Both couples work on rebounds, throw-ins, with team work for circle play. Centre court work on reaction time practices (see p. 7), plus giving and going skills.

Skill: Phase Three
Together, the whole team play a half-court game, attacks *vs.* defences, starting from a centre pass. The attacks score by goals. The defences score by interceptions, rebounds, and throw-ins, leading to a series of passes which should successfully reach the centre circle.

DURATION OF WARM-UP

In competitive situations it is vitally important that the coach considers not only what should be included in a warm-up, but also how long it should last, and what amount of rest should follow before the start of the match.

If a team spends too long in doing too vigorous a warm-up, then fatigue will set in and result in adverse effects on performance. It is therefore suggested that the length of a warm-up be such that it achieves some of the aims covered at the beginning of this chapter. A fifteen minute warm-up has been found to have more beneficial effects than those of shorter duration, and a warm-up period of between 15–30 minutes is therefore considered here to be sufficient for most players.

REST PERIOD BETWEEN WARM-UP AND GAME

It is generally accepted that anywhere between 5–10 minutes should be sufficient to allow the players to recover enough to be in an optimum physical condition to start the game. Much longer and the beneficial effects of warm-up will start to wear off.

It is the coach's responsibility to plan match tactics so that, if the event is running to time, the team start their warm-up approximately 30 minutes before the start of the match. In this way they would have a 20–25 minutes activity, followed by a 5–7 minute rest, before going onto the court ready to play.

N.B. The coach should also prepare her players to cope with any stoppages which might occur during play (e.g. as a result of an injury). It is a good idea to have a ball ready to give to the team so that they continue to keep warm and retain their awareness of the ball at competition pitch during any stoppage.

13
Set Pieces

CENTRE PASS

The centre pass is perhaps the most basic set piece of the game, and one that is usually introduced first. Play from a centre pass is normally the easiest way of scoring a goal because:

1 The player starts with possession, and therefore no energy or time is consumed in having to intercept the opposition's pass or shot.

2 The player will have the initiative in knowing which player will receive the pass, where she will receive it, how she will receive it, and who should receive it after her.

Given all this, however, it is nonetheless true that even at the highest level only about a third of centre passes result in a goal. Why?

The reasons are, more often than not, unforced errors. The ball is angled too far ahead of the receiver; the line is broken; or a feed into the circle places the shooters at a disadvantage. The centre pass is such an important move that it should be practised frequently against a variety of defending ploys. The system adopted for this pass should be flexible, with all players prepared and ready to respond to what might be a totally, unplanned move.

Communication

As well as verbal communication, teams can use signs and signals during a game. For example, there may be a set signal given by the goalkeeper and, when the team see it, they know who is to receive the first pass and, in consequence, how play will develop into the circle. The main problem with this method is that any lapse of memory on the part of signaller or team can result in chaos.

Rota systems

In rota systems a set order is adhered to in sequence. This can be, for instance, a constant repetition of:

1 *A word* (e.g. APPLE)   A = Goal Attack E = Wing Defence
                                 P = Wing attack L = Goal Defence
the centre starts at the beginning of the word and keeps repeating it through. This system is especially good with young players because they will enjoy making up new code word.

2 *A set order of passes.* For example, 'round the square', i.e. passes around the square created by the centre court markings. The centre may

start at any point on the square and follow it around clockwise or anti-clockwise. She can also:

— reverse the square,
— work diagonally across the square,
— double up on the square

In the latter, the centre has two systems. The first four centre passes go directly around the square, e.g. Wing Attack, Goal Attack, Wing Defence, Goal Defence. The fifth pass goes to the Wing Attack followed by the sixth, i.e. she has doubled-up. This is followed by single passes to the other three players. The next double is Goal Attack, and so on around the square. This system is effective, by requiring that players have good memories.

The one player system

This simply means that one player, most often the Wing Attack, is constantly used to receive the centre pass. This continues until the opposition stops her by using a double-up defence. In this eventuality, another pre-selected team member moves for the pass.

Centre pass patterns

The centre pass should not be considered completed until the ball is through the net for a goal. Therefore, the centre pass does not merely consist of the first pass, but also the subsequent pattern of play into the circle. There are certain basic principles which can be used as guidelines in planning the centre pass. These are attack, second pass, spatial plan and player plan.

Attack

The players should always try and ensure that the first move takes them towards their own goal. This means that players like the Goal Attack and Wing Attack should attempt to narrow their angle of movement so that they do not move too far down the centre court to receive the first pass. Goal Defence and Wing Defence should attempt to gain as much attacking ground as possible by receiving their pass ahead of the centre, and therefore nearer their own goal.

Second pass

The second pass is vitally important because any attacking player in a 1-v-1 situation should receive the first pass. This is not to say, however, that good defence play may not force her to receive it in a disadvantageous position. Also some defence systems (e.g. a zone, see ch. 11, p. 90) virtually allow the first pass to be received because the defending team have positioned themselves in such a way as to be able to pick off any subsequent pass. Who will receive the second pass, and where it is received, will be dictated by where the first pass is caught. It is important to have a basic plan that allows for flexibility rather than a rigid system of a specific player in a specific space.

Spatial plan

One method of achieving flexibility is by using a 'spatial plan'. What is meant by this is that if, for example, a Wing Attack moves to the right to take the pass, she will look to a player moving from somewhere *left* of the court to receive the next pass. A further example is if a player has been forced to take the ball in her defence area of the centre court, she would look to a player moving *out* of this area to take the next pass. This helps to ensure that all important attackers are not pulled away from the area the team is trying to reach, i.e. the attacking third.

Player plan

Rather than looking at *where* on the court a move is to be initiated, the team could plan *who* is to receive the second pass. In this case the succeeding player must be capable of reading the game well enough so that she can time her move in order that she can lose her opponent and use the space to make the thrower's task as easy as possible. The main problem with this plan is that if this player is not available, the team would have to adapt quickly and use someone else.

One tactic, which does not seem to be used often enough, is the 'one–two', or 'wall pass', to a centre who has been left free. If the opposing centre chooses to double-mark a particularly dangerous attacker, then the centre with the ball should distribute it quickly and move to take the return pass before her defender recovers her position.

STARTING POSITIONS

Where players start their move is obviously going to influence the efficiency of the action. Basically, what players should be attempting to do is to optimise their attacking possibilities whilst minimising the opposition's defence possibilities.

Where the player starts will obviously be dictated by what she feels she needs to do. For example, a player using a straight sprint would position herself up to the line and orientate towards the space into which she is going to move. If a player is not quick enough to out-sprint her opponent, more space and time is needed to effectively lose the opposition. In this case, she may start away from the line, thus giving herself the space to dodge and sprint, or change direction, or change speed and direction.

The starting position is also important in terms of creating space in which to move. For example, a Wing Attack who intends to use a straight sprint might start her move from the centre of the third line. *By the use of her feet* she can keep her opponent away from her space, and can also alter this space very quickly to counter any defence move. This can be done by adopting the starting position advocated in chapter 5 (see also Fig. 9).

One problem a player must beware of creating by her starting position is allowing herself to be forced into a disadvantageous position to receive her pass. For example, from the position in Figure 9 (ch. 5), she can be forced to receive her pass so near the side-line that any handling error may lead to a throw-in to the opposition. By making her angle to the line slightly wider, she can move out but slightly forward, and hence away from the side-line.

Each player should have the skills to be able to adapt flexibly to the demands of the game. Obviously every player has their own preferred way of moving but if this is not efficient in terms of dealing with her current opponent, then she must be capable of adapting.

Centre with ball

The rule governing the position of the centre in possession of the ball is that she be wholly inside the centre circle. The opposing centre should be in the centre third, and free to move.

Given that this is the case, and that the rule-governing obstruction indicates that a defender should come no closer than 3' distance from the attackers landing, grounded, or pivoting foot (or where she is grounded on both feet, the distance is measured from the nearer foot of the attacker to the nearer foot of the defender), it would seem logical that the centre in possession of the ball should adopt a symmetrical base as close to the edge of the circle as possible. This will mean that the defending centre will have to move 3' away from her, thus giving her the advantage of minimising chances of an interception and being fractionally nearer her own goal. From this position she can step in any direction and adopt a base which will allow efficient distribution of the ball even to the extent of, in a dire emergency, being able to pivot away from her goal and play safe by a back pass.

Defending centre

Basically the defending centre has four choices open to her, but the one she selects should depend on the team tactics being played and her own assessment of the situation:

1 She may adopt a tight man-to-man defence by covering the pass of her opponent and making it difficult for an accurate pass to be made. She might attempt an actual interception, but should not leave the ground as during the time she is in the air her opponent will have moved out of the circle and into attack. Having covered the first pass, she should then cover her opponent and attempt to prevent or delay her next contribution in the attacking play.

2 If one of the attacking players is proving dangerous and highly successful at the centre pass, she may choose to double-defend her. Having done this, and hopefully prevented the attack from receiving a centre pass, she should quickly return to defending her opponent. Or, if this is not viable, space mark in the attacking third and try to pick off the ball going into the circle.

3 She may space mark the attacking area of the centre court between Wing Attack and Goal Attack. Hopefully in this way she will prevent them

from moving into the central area of the court for this pass. By cooperation between the centre and her own defences, attacks can be forced so wide to the edge of the court that the pass will be very high risk and will therefore require greater accuracy on the part of the passing centre. From this position she is also in an advantageous place to cover the forward move into attack of her opposing centre.

4 If the team are playing a zone defence (see ch. 11, p. 90), she should start her move back on the third line and, on the whistle, drop back into the zonal position around the circle.

Other defending players

Basically these players should be looking to adopt a position which is going to minimise the attack's chances of success. Before the whistle there is often repositioning and 'jostling' for position, with attacking ploys being off-set by defensive counters. The defence should try to create a situation where the attack has:

1 As little space as possible in which to move.

2 A limited choice of space. For example, if a Wing Attack moves out towards the side-line before the whistle, and the Wing Defence is on her left, the Wing Attack can only really move forward, parallel to the side-line, thus cutting down the number of options open for the defence to cover.

3 To take the pass on her weaker hand.

Very often the defence has no chance of intercepting the first pass and her futile efforts to do so can create a position where her attacker may make an unopposed pass and then move off in attack. If the defence realises that this is the case, she should regulate her defensive move so that she is in a position to cover the pass made by her opponent and then make the next attacking move as difficult as possible. This is done by ensuring that, in her first attempt to intercept the centre pass, she does not finish her move but instead travels on ahead of the attacker and away from the goal she is defending.

TEACHING THE CENTRE PASS

As with the teaching of personal skills, the teaching of a tactic follows a *formula*; except that this time, because of the nature of the activity, the players do not start by working alone.

Following the formula, the players work from the simple to the complex, firstly working unopposed and gradually introducing opponents until a simulated game situation is reached.

Development stages

Stage 1: The first move
Playing Unit: Two (Feeder, Receiver).

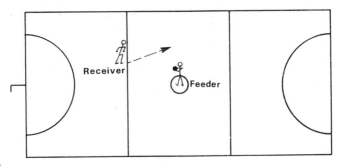

Fig. 46

Apparatus: One ball.
Starting position: See Figure 46.

Procedure
Using the idea developed in initiating motion (p. 26), the receiver stands ahead of the feeder, with her feet angled to either the right or left. The signal for the skill to start is given by the sender who tosses the ball in the air and regains possession. The receiver sprints out to whichever side she is facing and receives a pass. She lands, obeying the foot rule, pivots, if necessary, and returns the ball to the feeder.

This is repeated to both sides.

Stage 2: The fixed starting position
The playing unit and apparatus are as in stage 1 above, but this time the receiver is restricted in that she must start from behind a line (exactly as she would have to do for a centre pass). She must remain behind the line until the signal to start (as above) has been given. As with the first move, she travels to both right and left to receive the ball.

N.B. The position of the feet before the start is vital. For example, if the player wishes to move to the right, she should have her feet placed as shown in Figure 7 (ch. 5). This position allows the player to keep her opponent at least the distance of the width of her base away, and allows her to pivot quickly and easily to the left if her opponent re-positions to cover the space to the right. Having received a pass she lands, adjusts her base (as necessary) and throws back to the feeder.

Stage 3: The second pass
Playing Unit: Three (Goal Attack, Wing Attack, Centre).
Apparatus: One ball
Starting Unit: See Figure 47.

Procedure
The first move is initiated as in Figure 9 (ch. 5). On receiving the pass from the Centre, the Wing Attack pivots to face her own goal. The Goal Attack

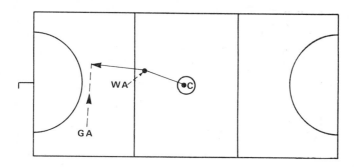

Fig. 47

who has positioned herself to the rear of the Wing Attack, crosses the opposite side of the court to receive the second pass.

N.B. As with stage 2, the Wing Attack works both to the right and the left, with the Goal Attack watching where she is going (by looking at the direction of her feet), adjusting her starting position accordingly, and moving from the opposite side of the court to receive the second pass.

When to move
The decision 'when to move' for the ball is vital for both the first receiver and succeeding players. Basically, the *first player* has two choices:

1 She may sprint off on the sound of the whistle; much the same as a sprinter at the start of a race. If she is faster than her opponent and is certain she can outsprint her, this would be the most straightforward decision to take.

2 If she is not certain about her sprinting ability, she should try to create uncertainty in her opponent by, for instance, delaying her sprint. The position of her body will have indicated to the opponent her intended direction. Therefore, her main advantage is temporal—*when* she is to move. By delaying her sprint by as much as one second (approximately) after the whistle, she will have created uncertainty in her opponent who may have relaxed, thinking the ball is to go elsewhere. A sudden late sprint *should* leave the player clear to collect the pass.

The succeeding players have a far more difficult job. They have to make their *final* move when the preceding player is ready to throw. This is often very hard to do, particularly if that player jumps high in the air to receive the pass. In this case, the next player would have to wait for the receiver to land and, if necessary, pivot and adjust the throwing base, counter her opponent's position, and throw. Often the next player moves into the correct space too soon and, by the time the ball is ready to be sent, she will be defended, making it necessary for her to move to another space. This invariably wastes both time and energy. If the player (particularly the young, or highly anxious) has difficulty in determining when to move, it may be that for a period of time she should play undefended, with the coach giving a verbal cue to her as to when she should make her move. However, before the player becomes too dependent upon these cues she must be helped to select those that allow her to decide for herself the correct time to make her final move.

Stage 4: The third pass

Playing Unit: Four (Centre, Wing Attack, Goal Attack, Goal Shooter).
Apparatus: One ball and place bibs.
Starting position: See Figure 48.

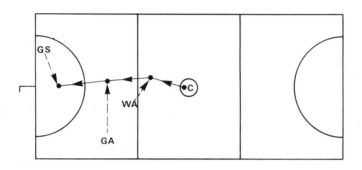

Fig. 48

Procedure
The players form an attacking unit of: Centre, Wing Attack, Goal Attack, Goal Shooter.

Play proceeds as in the previous development stages, but this time the third player (GS) positions herself in the shooting circle: her brief being to move for the ball in a position within the circle from which she is most accurate. This will mean that the second player will have to select the correct pass to reach her in that position.

N.B. Each time the shooter receives the ball *she must shoot* and, hit or miss, move in for the rebound.

MOVEMENT OFF THE BALL

After the above stages have been reached, movement off the ball should be coached. Given that there is no opposition, players should be coached to *throw and go,* i.e. pass the ball and move off into the *free space.* Thus the movement of the whole sequence might be as Figure 49 A,B.

The Centre and Wing Attack now learn to back-up the circle, and the Goal Attack quickly gets into the circle to back-up the Goal Shooter; either by a rebound jump to gain possession, or by receiving a wall-pass from the Goal Shooter which should bring her nearer to the goal for an easier shot.

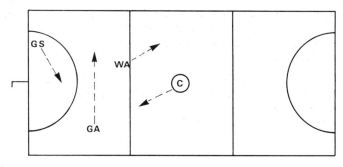

Fig. 49A

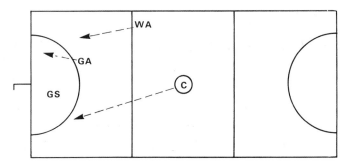

Fig. 49B

Opposition

When players 'movement off the ball' has reached a higher level of skill, opposition should be gradually introduced. If, for instance, four opponents are put in immediately, every skill will disintegrate in the players' efforts to get free, and therefore little reinforcement of what has been learnt will take place. The type and sequence of opposition that may be used is set out below. It should be noted, however, that the player with the easiest job is Wing Attack. She knows when and where she intends to move. She is a decision-maker and, at this simple level, not dependent on reading cues from other players, i.e. the Centre has no opponent.

The first opponent is Wing Defence
Her task is to mark the first move of Wing Attack. If she fails to intercept the first pass, she should position herself ready to cover the pass to Goal Attack. Goal Attack would now have to adjust her move to help Wing Attack make a successful pass, and would therefore also need to decide not only when to move, but where, in relation to her own player and the opposition, is the best space to use.

The second opponent is Goal Defence
The tactic should develop as above, but there will obviously now be more

decisions to be made by the player. At this stage, if the Goal Attack cannot get free to receive the second pass, the Wing Attack may be asked (by the coach) to use one of the two free players on the court (Centre and Goal Shooter) to allow Goal Attack more time to get free and receive the third pass.

The third opponent is Goal-Keeper
When this stage arises the players will be forced into making more realistic decisions. They should know the optimum way to get the ball into a shooting position, but would now be forced to sacrifice this to get the ball *safely* into the circle. They can and should be encouraged to use other players (e.g. the free Centre) to open up the game to create time and space for the circle players to gain the best position possible to shoot.

The fourth opponent is the opposing centre
This opponent is left until last. The reason for this is that her presence may mean that a tactic may not get started because, by her marking of the first pass, the Wing Attack may not be able to receive the ball and, hence, frustration will ensue.

N.B. In these initial stages the opposing centre should only mark the pass and not double 'mark' Wing Attack.

When the players are at this stage, the Goal Attack may then be used as an alternative for the first pass. This will be made necessary if the Centre is free to mark where she wishes and, by double-marking the Wing Attack, forces the attackers to use Goal Attack.

N.B. Players should be taught that if the Centre chooses to do this and unless she is very quickly back to marking her own opponent, the attacking Centre may well be used for a *very quick* return or wall-pass from Goal Attack.

SUMMARY
The centre pass to any players can be taught as follows:
1 Where to start.
2 Where to move.
3 When to move.
4 To whom should the second pass be made.
5 Where to go when you have passed.

Remember with centre passes, as with the rest of the game, *KISS*—Keep It Simple Stupid. There is little to be gained by complicated doubling-up systems of blocking-in the player who is to make the first move. So often, particularly with younger players, this causes confusion for the attackers rather than the defenders. What needs to be taught here is to use the attacking players in the simplest way possible to get free for a centre pass, i.e. a sprint. The same method can also be applied by using the defending players and adopting a feint dodge, change of speed, or change of direction, as means of defeating an opponent and being free to receive a pass.

14
Full Court Play

HORIZONTAL BANDING

Horizontal banding is the division of the court into seven bands that correspond to seven players (see Fig. 50). It is one of the simplest ways available for teaching full court play, with each player being responsible for the passage of the ball through her band, or, if the long high pass is used, over her area of the court.

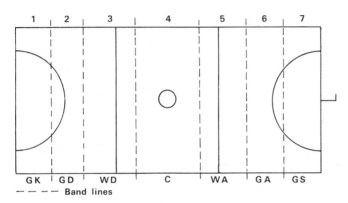

Fig. 50

Development stages

These are initially taught without opposition.

Stage 1

Procedure
A number of balls are given to the Goal-Keeper, who places them along the goal-line (see Fig. 51).

The Goal-Keeper then starts the move by selecting any ball at random and passing it to the appropriate player. Each player starts and finishes her move and receives the ball *in her own band* (see Fig. 52).

Where she starts
This will depend on the starting position of the succeeding player, which is dictated by where the Goal-Keeper puts the ball into play. Basically, players move from side-line to mid-court, starting opposite each other with the ball moving straight down mid-court. The goal defence has one extra

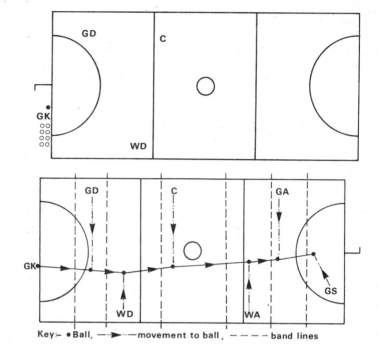

Fig. 51

Fig. 52   Key:- ●Ball, ─··▶···movement to ball, ─ ─ ─ ─ band lines

prohibition: she has a 'no-go' area in the defending circle where she may not attempt to receive the ball (see Fig. 53). The reason for this is that any mishandling in this area would lead to a fairly safe shot at goal for the opposition.

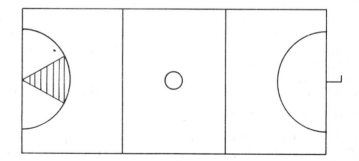

Fig. 53

When to start
The timing of each move should be such that the receiver moves only when the succeeding player has possession of the ball and is herself ready to throw. The full court sequence would therefore be: GK, GD, WD, C, WA, GA, GS.

Each player starts, finishes and receives in her own band.

Stage 2

Procedure

Players start off, but finish and receive within their band. This should result in a more realistic spatial patterning of moves, although again the passage of the ball should be as direct as possible. At this stage the coach can add conditions so that, for instance, players:

1 Show a change of speed when going for the ball.

2 Show a dodge before receiving the ball.

3 Show a change of direction before receiving the ball.

This will add further realism to the situation and help to eliminate the constant 'one speed' running seen in so many team attacks.

Stage 3 Role interchange

In theory, bands only correspond to players, but, in reality, the ball should be passed to the more advantageously-placed player who, for tactical reasons, may be well away from her own theoretical band. In such cases the players change roles and adopt the playing role of the band in which they receive the ball. For example, if the Centre cannot receive a pass in band 4, because she is too heavily defended, she moves out and leaves the band empty. If Wing Attack moves in to this empty band, it should be to play a Centre's role, i.e. the mid-field link. The Centre now moves into band 5 and plays a Wing Attack, whose primary role is to feed the circle.

To simulate this role interchange in a team working without opposition, the coach dictates who is 'marked out' and not available for a pass in their correct band.

The ball is then put into play as above and, as this happens, the coach calls the position which is 'marked out'. For example, 'Wing Defence marked out'. In this situation, the Centre moves into band 3 and plays 'Wing Defence'. In the meantime, Wing Defence moves ahead into band 4 and links attack and defence by playing 'Centre'. Any player may be called, except the player putting the ball into play. As the team becomes more adept, two players may be called. For example, Goal Defence and Goal Shooter. In the above case, Wing Defence receives the first pass with Goal Defence filling band 3. At the other end, Goal Shooter leaves the circle and feeds Goal Attack who has moved in to take her place and shoot for goal.

Stage 4 With opposition

As with the centre pass, opposition is introduced gradually, starting with Goal Shooter—thus making the initial pass more difficult and possibly altering the positioning of the whole team. One player at a time is introduced until all seven are marked and a full game situation is being simulated.

TWO METHODS OF ORGANISATION

Most coaches and teachers will have two teams to deal with—often with too few balls and too little space. Two suggestions are made to deal with this situation:

Method 1
This first method can be rather static, but it should help in the initial stages of organising teams, particularly if players are having difficulty with timing.

Team A   takes up positions on the court to start, receive and finish within their own band.

Team B   stands to the side of the court, each player standing adjacent to the band they would be in if on court.

Team B's Goal-Keeper calls 'play', as this happens, Team B's Goal Defence calls 'Goal Defence'. On this signal, the Goal Defence on court moves for the pass. She may *not* move until the signal has been given, i.e. the Goal-Keeper is ready to throw the ball. Each player off court calls the name of the player on court, and this is her signal to move. Both teams must be aware of what is happening because if a player in Team B forgets the signal, play will break down. Obversely, if a player in Team A moves before the signal is called, she has *probably* over-anticipated and will therefore move too soon for the thrower. In this way *it is hoped* the team off-court will be learning by observing, and the team on court receiving some help with the difficult skill of timing.

Method 2
This second method is more active, using greater spatial restrictions and hence a higher degree of control on the part of the players.
    The court is divided longitudinally, as shown in Figure 54, into Team 'A' and 'B'

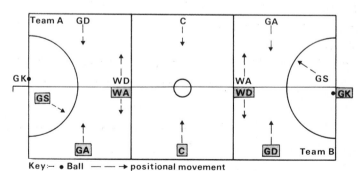

Fig. 54   Key:— ● Ball — — → positional movement

When Team 'A' Goal Shooter has shot, Team 'B' Goal-Keeper retrieves the ball, calls 'play', and the ball is then passed through Team 'B' to the Goal Shooter. Following her shot, the ball is collected by Team 'A' Goal-Keeper, who puts it into play for her team. Using this method, *a minimum* of two balls is needed; and yet it is possible to have a great deal of constructive activity on the court.

Pressure training

' Using the idea of a team starting out of their band, but finishing and receiving in it (plus players being 'marked out'), added pressure can be imposed as follows:

Using as many balls as possible behind the defensive goal-line and side-lines to the point of the first third, the player throwing-in selects any ball and calls 'play'. The succeeding players have selected where to start, based on her position. As soon as the first pass has been received the next ball is put into play from a different position. This means that players have constantly to distribute the ball and readjust their position relative to the starting position of the ball. Further pressure is added by the role interchange required when a player is 'marked out' of play by the call of the coach.

VERTICAL BANDING

This can be used to:

1 Teach spacing to beginners, or teams who are crowding.

2 Emphasise the importance of width of attack with more skilful teams.

Task One: The brick wall
The court is divided longitudinally by a 'brick wall'.

Condition on play
The ball and the Centre only may pass through the wall. All other players are restricted to receiving the ball on either side, depending on their position. This may also be taught as longitudinal 'tram-lines' with only players having to work within their own set of lines. In this way the clustering of players around the player with the ball may be prevented.

Task Two: Width of attack

Condition on play
Here the band down the centre is extended in width (see Fig. 55). The ball

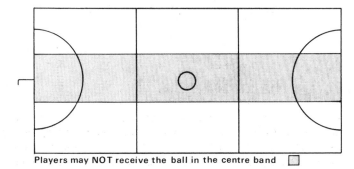

Fig. 55   Players may NOT receive the ball in the centre band   ☐

may not be received in this area, but players may travel through it to move into a space which will open up play. By increasing the width of attack, the attackers are giving the defenders a greater area of space to cover. As a general rule, defenders prefer to narrow space and time when ball is in the air. This gives them the most advantageous position. Therefore, by increasing the space covered, and decreasing the time the ball is in that space, the attackers are putting extra pressure on the defence.

SIDE AND GOAL-LINE THROW-IN

The rule

When the ball goes out of court, it must be put into play by a member of the opposing team either by:

1 The player who last had contact with the ball.

2 The player who received the ball with any part of her touching the ground outside the court.

The player throwing in the ball must:

1 Stand outside the court and place one foot as close as possible to the line, without touching or standing on it, at the point where the Umpire indicates that the ball has crossed the line.

2 Throw only from behind a line bounding her own playing area.

The tactic

This rule means that a team has a large degree of discretion as to which player brings the ball into play. There are some factors which the team needs to consider when making this decision:

1 The position on the court where the throw is to be taken.

2 The ability of players to throw accurately under pressure.

3 The strengths and weaknesses of the opposition.

4 The ability of her own team.

5 The space available on the court.

Having made the decision as to who is taking the throw-in, the next problem is what tactic the players on court should adopt. One method of cutting down on any indecision is to have a *basic plan* which operates irrespective of the players involved. *One example* of this type of plan is when the player nearest the thrower remains in that space until the command 'play'. She then moves out and allows the next nearest player to move into the space which has been vacated. By this 'screening' of the space until the very last moment, the attacking team is ensuring that the throw-in will have the minimum distance to travel, and hence cut down on the possible variables which might lead to error.

PENALTIES

The rule

Penalties, with the exception of the throw-up, *are awarded to a team.* A penalty for an infringement on court is taken where the infringement occurred, except where this puts the non-offending team at a disadvantage, in which case, the penalty shall be taken where the contacted or obstructed player was standing. For example, if a penalty shot should be taken from directly under the post, it may be taken from where the original shot was taken.

The tactic

Again it is left to the discretion and speed of decision-making of the offended team as to which player takes the penalty. There are several factors which must be taken into account:

The speed of taking the penalty
This has both positive and negative aspects. The positive aspect is that, by taking the penalty quickly, the offended team may catch the opposition defence out of position and be able to capitalise on this.

The negative side is that this same speed may, in certain circumstances, do the same to their own team. For example, attacks who have gone down the court to zone in front of the defence third will have a great deal of ground to cover to be back in their own area of play if the penalty is taken too quickly. Each situation must therefore be seen as a unique occurrence and dealt with in the most appropriate way.

Releasing the most useful player
When a penalty is awarded to a team, any player may take it. It is to the advantage of the team to allow a player with 'little' attacking potential to take the penalty, thus releasing other players who can make a more positive contribution to the game. An example would be if a Goal Attack is fouled by her opposing Goal Defence outside the circle. By allowing the Wing Attack or a Centre to take the pass the attackers have a 2:1 overlap in the circle by the Goal Defence being obliged to stand by the player making the pass, thus making for an easy scoring opportunity.

A PENALTY PASS OR SHOT?

This very much depends on where in the circle the offence took place. Given that the non-offending defender is free to attempt to defend, either of the attackers should take whichever is going to create the most problems for the defence. If the offence occurred away from the post, the free defender should either cover the free shooter to prevent the pass (or space mark) and hope to distract the shooter by her presence, and also have a chance to cut-off any pass which may be made. Nearer to the post, where the shot is relatively easy, she may attempt an interception knowing that she is near enough for a rebound chance.

In either of these situations, the shooters should try the unexpected. A 'shot' will be very hard to counter if, at the last minute it becomes a pass over the head of the defence, or is moved swiftly down to be bounced through the feet to the other shooter. It must be emphasised that speed, and the element of surprise, are essential. In these circumstances an understanding between the two shooters is essential because the team who sees a penalty wasted by the ball bouncing off the other shooter, who was not ready to receive a pass, is going to be very frustrated. Where possible, e.g. when the other defence is not blocking the passage to goal, a step-up shot is most useful as it decreases the distance between shooter and goal and, hence, increases the chance of scoring.

THE THROW-UP

The rule

Rules concerning throw-up are far too long for inclusion here, but can be found in the *Official Netball Rules* (by A.E.N.A). It is most *essential* that players know and understand these rules because the throw-up is awarded to the player and not the team. The player concerned may not take the throw-up because to do so would infringe the territorial rules. Therefore, any two opposing players permitted in that area may take it.

The tactic

The stance
Players vary in the type of stance they prefer. However, most adopt a base where one foot is in front of the other. In the early stages, players should experiment leading with right or left foot, and also with a symmetrical base. At an advanced level, the player will have considered where she is going to pass the ball when she is successful, and will adopt a base which will make the next pass most efficient, i.e. she will not have to adjust the base to make the pass.

Arms in line with body
The arms must be in line with the sides of the body and should be held with a degree of tension that will allow them to be moved as quickly as possible. The hands should be open, with the fingers slightly spread to fasten around the ball.

Attention
Once the player has assessed the situation with regard to her own team and the opposition, she should concentrate wholly on the point where the ball rests on the umpire's hand. This is where the first motion will occur and it is important that players respond to this first visual cue rather than wait for the sound of the whistle.

Actions on contacting the ball
Immediately on contacting the ball the grip should increase and the arms continue the upsweeping action which took them away from the sides and

towards the ball. This action should continue upwards and *away from the direction of the opponent,* and be accompanied by a twisting of the trunk. This action not only takes the ball away from the opponent, but can also act as the preparatory action for the succeeding throw.

If the throw-up is lost

The player should immediately cover the throw, or shot. What she does depends on the area of the court in which play is taking place. If in the circle, a shooter who wins a throw-up may shoot and therefore the defender will probably attempt an interception. If, for example, it is won by an attacking player well down the centre court, the defender should cover the pass, but *not* leave the ground. If she failed to deflect the pass, she should immediately cover the 'attackers' move down the court.

The position of the other players

The other players must be aware of the space on the court and, should the throw-up be won, which of them is in the most advantageous position to receive a pass. They may not receive a pass themselves, but, by creating space, they will allow a better placed player to move in for the ball. Players must also be aware of the position of their opponents and the space they have available because, should the opposition win the throw-up, they would have to immediately adopt a defensive role.

Coaching the throw-up

When coaching the tactic for the throw-up, the following points are important:

1 Vary the 'umpire' so that players do not get used to only one type of throw-up. It is important that where a specific umpire is to be used for a match or tournament, the players should be accustomed to her timing.

2 Vary the side in which the ball is put into play. Sometimes players are faster when the ball is put in on their preferred hand. It is therefore important that they work on both sides of the body.

3 When practising throw-ups, players should work in realistic units. For example, Wing Attack opposing Wing Defence with Goal Attack and Goal Defence each ready to take the succeeding pass from the winner.

The development stages in achieving the above skill may be as follows:

Stage 1
Playing Unit: Three
Apparatus: One ball

Two players stand facing each other and their goals, as specified in the rules. The third player acts as the 'umpire'. The 'umpire' puts the ball into play, varying which side of the two players she stands. The two players vary their stance and attempt to find which is the most efficient position for them personally. Each player attempts to snatch the ball before the opponent, and pull it away from the space where the opponent is positioned. Each player should act as both 'umpire' and opponent.

Stage 2

Playing Unit: Three

Apparatus: One ball

Play commences as stage 1, but the 'umpire', having put the ball into play, acts as a third player and moves to receive a pass from the successful player. The unsuccessful player should attempt to cover the ball and intercept the pass. The successful player must then make a pass which will avoid this defence, while the 'umpire' should ask for the pass in a space which will help the sender to achieve this end, i.e. one which will not have to pass through the space covered by the defence.

Stage 3

Playing Unit: Five

Apparatus: One ball and place bibs.

The skill proceeds as in stage 2, but with a further two opponents ready to adopt an attacking or defensive role depending on the result of the throw-up. At this stage, players should be working in compatible units and the two players taking part in the throw-up should be aware of the position of the other two players, both in relation to the throw-up and the space available on the court. The players ready to receive or defend a pass should attempt to make their judgements based on:

1 Whether the umpire is putting the ball into play on their player's fastest side.

2 How their player is standing. Is her base such that she will be able to throw without adjustment, or will she need to move her feet before she can make a pass.

3 How she can best move to avoid the covering defence.

4 How, if necessary, can she quickly adjust to a defensive role.

These judgements will be based on previous experience, as well as on the current events. Teams should know those players who are fast reactors and are most likely to win every throw-up. This will assist the team in adopting a more attacking position because of the likelihood of a throw-up being successful. Throw-ups should be practised in every area of the court with each team member, at some stage, being involved in the throw-up.

By constant repetition the team will develop a positive attitude to throw-ups and, by so doing, react quickly and efficiently to the re-start of play. This type of work can be covered by two teams playing a normal game, but with the coach synthesising throw-up situations at any time and at any position on the court. These throw-ups should not only be taken between two positional opponents, but also between two unrelated players. For example Team A's Wing Attack and Team B's Goal Defence outside the circle. In this way, players will have to quickly adjust their positions to cope with the result.

N.B. In all throw-up situations the players should be conditioned to immediately defend if the ball is not won.

15
Fitness and Training

Training should not simply consist of ball skills and team play, but incorporate an 'all the year round' fitness programme. Whatever the ability of a player, she can only do justice to her full potential if she is in 'peak' condition. Every individual is different, and it is only through experimentation that a player will discover her own 'recipe' for fitness.

For a training process to have any meaning, the various demands of the game must be evaluated so as to help players adapt to them. There are six fundamental ingredients which need to be considered when devising a training programme. These are often referred to as the six 'S's—stamina, speed, strength, skill, suppleness, (p)sychology. Where the emphasis is placed will depend on (1) the playing position, (2) the individual's strengths and weaknesses and (3) whether it is in or out of the competitive season.

STAMINA

The ability to play well in the last five minutes depends on stamina. One way this may be achieved is regular, steady, even-paced running over 1 to 3 miles. A more valuable exercise for the netball player is 'speed-play' running, which involves continual changes of pace, i.e. sprinting, striding,

Table 3   Circuit training

	Exercises	Repetitions	Laps	Times per week
	Trunk curls (abdominal muscles)	10	Initially two—increase	Two or three
	Squat jumps (leg power)	8	to three	
	Dorsal raises (back muscles)	8	as fitness improves	
	Press-ups (arm power)	Maximum		
	Step-ups (leg power)	10 each leg		
	Salmon snaps (abdominal muscles)	10		
	Squat thrusts (leg power)	8		

jogging and walking. Each change of speed can be over short (30 yards) or long (200 yards) distances, and the total covered may vary in length from 1 to 3 miles, depending on basic fitness of the individual. Another and perhaps more 'popular' way of achieving 'staying power' is circuit training. This is a series of repetitive exercises which ensure that *all* the body parts are exercised. Having decided which exercises are of most value to the netball player, care must be taken to put them in a sensible order so that one body part is not exercised successively. An example of a circuit which may be done is set out in Table 3. Here the training dose is fixed but, where possible, individual numbers of maximum repetitions should be worked out.

Like all forms of training, circuits must to be done *regularly* if they are to be of value. Each time the circuit is performed, the time should be recorded to act as a target to be beaten at the next session.

SPEED

The ability to out-sprint an opponent depends on speed. It is important to remember that the ability to accelerate quickly over a short distance is often very valuable in netball. This may be improved in several ways by using the netball court as the 'track'; the following tasks illustrate this.

Task One
Players sprint across the court, and jog back (see Fig. 56).

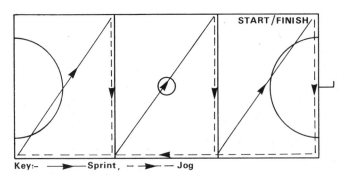

Fig. 56   Key:— ———▶———Sprint, – –▶ – – Jog

Repeat the above 3 times; rest for one minute; 3 more times; 1 minute rest; then 3 more times.

Task Two
Players start at A, finish at B and walk back to A (see Fig. 57). Repeat 3 times; alternate jogging and sprinting.

Task Three
As shown in Figure 58, the player sprints path 1 at full speed; walks (or jogs) back to start-line; sprints path 2 and so on.

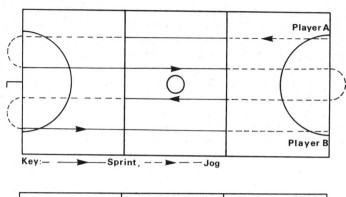

Fig. 57   Key:— ——————Sprint, — — ▶ — —Jog

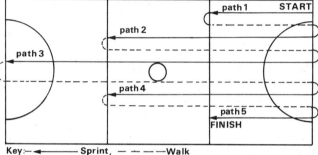

Fig. 58   Key:—◀————— Sprint, — — — —Walk

STRENGTH

The ability to handle the body and the ball more efficiently requires strength. Working against a resistance can help to improve this power, which in turn helps the player to jump higher, accelerate faster and throw harder. This can be achieved by working against a load and running or hopping, for example, up a slope or steps, instead of on level ground.

1 Harness running in the gymnasium (Fig. 59). Skipping rope is looped over the shoulders and under the arms; the rear runner gives resistance against which the player runs.

2 At home: running or hopping up the stairs (Fig. 60).

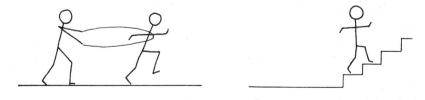

Fig. 59   Fig. 60

Strength may also be increased by using weights. As part of their closed and pre-season training, players should adapt to weights through circuits. After 4 weeks of circuit work, the adaptation process should be sufficient to allow safe use of weights. A suggested schedule could be:

Weeks 1–4:   Circuits
Weeks 5–8:   Weights done in conjunction with circuit training.

There are many weight training exercises, but some are more relevant for netball players. For example:

1 *Power clean.* A general power builder and excellent for major muscle groups.

2 *Front squats.* For the development of the anterior aspect of the thigh, also for hip muscles. This exercise is better for the thighs than back squats, and is safer for novices.

3 *Split squats.* For leg strength and mobility of the adductors.

4 *Press behind neck* (seated). Development of the shoulder, upper back, triceps and side of the chest.

5 *Upright rowing.* For shoulders, upper back and biceps.

6 *Sit-ups* (knees bent). Abdominals.

7 *Side bends.* Side of the trunk and mid section.

Before players attempt weight training, it is advisable to consult an expert to demonstrate the correct techniques. Lifting weights correctly and safely requires skill and practice. Contrary to myths, regular weight training will not turn ordinary players into 'muscle' men; nor will it change female muscles into male muscles. It is a very worthwhile and satisfying form of training.

(For further information on all the above exercises see *Know the Game 'Weight Training'*: Educational Publication.)

Many Sports Centres now have poly- or multi-gyms in their conditioning rooms. These are multi-stationed weight training machines which are so designed that an individual can follow a programme to exercise different muscle groups at each successive station. Most of these gyms have diagrammatic examples of programmes to be followed for different fitness aims. Many coaches will argue that these static weight stations do not provide the same degree of training as the more dynamic form done with sets of moveable weights. However, one of the advantages of this type of training is that it is very safe, and one can quite safely train alone. Despite this, it is always advisable to seek the help and advice of an expert to check such things as the position of apparatus relevant to height and reach and the range of movement being worked.

SUPPLENESS

A good range of movement is a valuable 'buffer' against injury and helps in reaching for those 'impossible' interceptions. There are two kinds of flexibility: static and dynamic. It is the latter which is of most use to netball players. A modern and popular way of increasing mobility is 'Popmobility'. This is a series of exercises performed to modern records, and entails repetitive routines through a full range of movement working on the different muscles and joints of the body. (There are several tapes and records available made specifically for this form of training, *see* Appendix.) Whilst this may be seen as a useful adjunct to achieving flexibility, the player should also work daily on a routine of exercises such of those found in *Mobility Exercises for Athletes,* P.R. Harper, BAAB Publications, 1971.

SKILL

Skill is the ability to perform all the functions required in netball with efficiency, effectiveness and consistency. It is necessary to assess what 'specific' skills are needed for each position, e.g. the Goal Shooter must be able to score goals as well as develop the general skills needed by every player. As a skill is learnt, various nerve pathways are laid down. Once established, they are never forgotten. This is one reason why repetitive practices, especially for the basic skills, are extremely important. It is also vital that 'correct' patterns are established from the start because it is far more difficult to remedy mistakes later. An enjoyable way of practising skill under pressure is to work through a skills circuit; an example of which is shown in Figure 61.

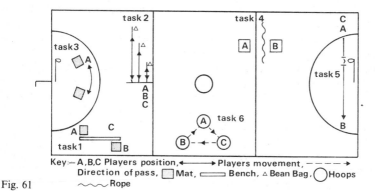

Key:— A,B,C Players position, ◄────► Players movement, ─ ─ ─ ─ ►
Direction of pass, ☐ Mat, ▭ Bench, △ Bean Bag, ◯ Hoops
Fig. 61   〜〜〜 Rope

The following six tasks illustrated in Figure 61 are carried out in groups. Each task should take 3 minutes, with each group keeping their own score. After 3 minutes one player from each group reports the total to the scorer (coach) and the groups then move onto the next task.

Task One

Three players, working in pairs, stand on either side of a bench and pass the ball parallel to it. The players then lean over the bench to catch the ball. Player C changes with Player A after one minute, then Player A changes with Player B for a further minute.

Task Two
Three players: Player A collects the bean bags (one at a time) and Player B puts them out again. Player C collects them and Player A puts them out again, and so on.

Task Three
Three players: Player A shoots alternatively from the 2 mats positioned as shown in Figure 61. Player B and C retrieve them. After one minute, Player B changes with Player A, and repeats the task; and so on.

Task Four
Three players: Same procedure as in task one, but overhead passes are made over-a rope supported by two high jump stands.

Task Five
Two players: Player A runs, jumps to touch the net, and finishes run. Player B repeats.

Task six
Three players: Three hoops positioned as in Figure 61. Each player has one foot in the hoop and they shoulder pass between each other.

(P)SYCHOLOGY

Human behaviour is highly individual and enormously complex. Success in sport can help many people to 'find themselves', but, unfortunately, there are others who allow failure to crush them. Each player has a unique genetic and environmental history, and must be considered as an individual. Everyone is born into a different environment and, by the time a youngster reaches the age for participation in formalised netball sessions, she has already developed a personality and psychological make-up that is fairly resistant to change. Without wishing to over-simplify this extremely complex and difficult area, it is possible to select two methods which may be used to aid human learning and performance. A good coach will try to focus mainly on the positive aspects of performance *before* analysing the faults.

A balance between error correction and reinforcing good performance is essential. For a coach whose team has a losing record, there is the problem of getting the players psychologically prepared to play well; in contrast, the 'winning' coach would need to carefully examine her schedule to pinpoint the games she believes the team are best prepared for psychologically. If she tries to get the team 'up' for every game, she may be unable to get that little extra from her team in a particularly crucial game. Similar situations arise in class teaching, where the less able pupils need encouragement to work on their basic skills. This is often achieved by using a whole series of different practices to achieve the same objective. With the more able, the problem is often to supply a sufficiently challenging situation to keep them motivated.

One method is to involve the players in devising their own skills and practices—a good way for the coach to also increase her own repertoire. The treatment of players during practices can produce strong positive, or negative, psychological benefits for a team. It may even be necessary to eliminate a player solely because of the potential psychological damage her presence might bring to the team. Some of the best coaches are also good 'psychologists'—knowing when to apply pressure and provide support.

FITNESS REQUIREMENTS ACCORDING TO POSITION

Each playing position has its own specific requirements and it is therefore necessary to select the work which is most appropriate. It must be pointed out that *all netball players should be 'athletes'*. In experiments carried out recently (using telemetry to assess in-game heart rate) it was found that netball is comparable with some of the most strenuous sports; with heart rates of 170+ beats per minute sustained for relatively long periods of time. Therefore, players need a high level of basic fitness to maintain this work rate.

Getting fit is *not* easy. It requires determination, perserverance and the will to succeed, but the subsequent benefits from being fit will easily compensate the player for her endeavours. Taking two specific positions—Goal Shooter and Centre—the fitness training differences are highlighted. It is senseless to make both players follow the same programme when their requirements are so obviously different.

Both players must practise their individual skills and work alongside their team-mates during match practice. However, there are also other forms of training which may form a valuable part of any players programme (see Table 4).

The time allotted for fitness training should be divided between the three types of training. The three types of training outlined in Table 4 are not very time-consuming, and only the weight training requires any apparatus. To reach peak fitness, a top player must train daily—as is the case with all major international sportsmen and women. However, the average club or school player may not be willing to give up that amount of time, but she should be encouraged to train as regularly as possible. If it is decided to combine fitness and skill training in one session, then work on a skill should *precede* the fitness training, whenever possible.

It is often easy to neglect fitness because players can be far more enthusiastic about actually playing a game. However by using competition, partner work, or work to music, the 'pill may be sugared' and the players should begin to enjoy their new found fitness to the full.

Most sportswomen keep a training diary, and this should be encouraged for all players. It could briefly include:

1 The number of competitive matches.

Table 4   Training differences for Goal Shooter and Centre

Position	Requirements		Training
Goal Shooter	Power:	to spring	Power—weight training
		to control the body at full extension	
		to control the ball with fingers and wrists	Shuttle running (short runs in a confined space)
	Agility:	to manoeuvre quickly within a confined space	Flexibility exercises.
	Stamina:	to maintain 100% concentration throughout the match	Circuit training, plus skill/endurance training.
		to perform her skills well (particularly shooting), even under pressure and at the end of an hours match	
		to keep alert and working in defence and attack during the game	
Centre	Stamina:	to maintain a high performance level for one hour.	Out of season 'speed play' over 1½–2 miles, with much 'fast' work.
	Speed:	to out-manoeuvre an opponent.	Short, fast repetitions using the court.
		to cover a court from end to end.	Circuit training and high quality speed shuttles.
		to mark and intercept.	
	Power:	to spring	Weight training.
		to control the body at speed.	

2 The level of the competition: School/Club/College/County/International.

3 The position played.

4 Whether the team won or lost, and the final score.

5 The amount and type of training, with times or pulse rates where necessary.

6 If the player is injured; what type of injury had she sustained? How long had she missed her training? What treatment was given?

VARIATIONS IN TRAINING ACCORDING TO TIME OF YEAR

Training schedules should vary according to the time of year and the level of competition. Two examples of schedules for advanced players are set out below and can be adapted to suit most teams. *Schedule One* is a form of 'topping-off', aimed at bringing the team to a physical 'peak' at the time of competition. *Schedule Two* is planned to last over a 2 month period and demands that players do some form of physical activity each day.

Schedule One: Pre-competition peakness

Training should be for 4 days per week in a gymnasium, if possible. Start each session with players jogging continuously around the court or gymnasium for at least 6 minutes. Follow this with general mobilising activities, e.g. shoulder circling, neck circling, trunk circling. (Examples may be taken from Mobility Exercises, P.R. Harper, B.A.A.B. Publication 1971.)

Day 1 Speed and endurance work—Shuttle running
Distance: 50 feet.
Number of runs: 10.
Rest period: 15 seconds
Number of repetitions: 4.
Complete recovery, and repeat twice more.

Day 2 Circuit training
Tasks are shown in Figure 61, and further explained on p. 125-6.

Day 3 Power drills, or skill and power circuits
These may be done on alternate weeks to add variety to training. In these drills the player must not be fatigued when starting the next activity and she should therefore take full recovery between exercises.

Power drills
Activities include:
— Hopping: The full length of the gymnasium; hop down on the right leg; walk back; hop on the left; walk back.
— Bounding: (2' to 2') bound the full length of the gymnasium; walk back.
— Striding: Exaggerated bounding strides –concentrate on the quick pick-up of the knee of the leading leg and drive off the rear leg.

Skill and power circuit
This is a series of activities alternating circuit training exercises with skill practices relevant to the player's position. For example, a Goal Shooter may do the following:
— 20 shots at goal from varying distances.
— 10 squat jumps.
— 20 chest passes against the wall.
— 10 salmon snaps.
— 20 alternate hand/wall passes.
— 10 tuck jumps.
— 20 high overhead snatches.
— 6 shuttle runs.

Day 4 Endurance
Distance: Full court.
Speed and endurance work: Sprint goal line—third line and back.
                                     Sprint goal line—second third line and back.
                                     Sprint goal line—goal line.
Recovery: 1½ minutes.
Repetitions: 4 times.
Heart rate is a more accurate form of recovery, the player should take her pulse (immediately on stopping) which should be over 150 beats/min. As soon as the pulse rate has slowed to about 120 beats/min, the player may start again. However, if this is not possible, a set recovery period must be given.

Schedule Two: Daily activity
This programme is divided into 7 days, including 2 matches:
Day 1: Match (results and position played recorded in training diary)
Day 2: Run 1½/2 miles, vary the terrain but the distance should not change so that an accurate record of times can be kept.
Day 3: Circuit training.
Day 4: Shuttles and bounds.
Day 5: Skill and endurance
Day 6: Circuit training.
Day 7: Rest or match or gentle run (2/3 miles).
The skill and endurance work will vary according to the player's position. The following examples are for shooters, defences and centre court:

Shooters

Task One
Three players positioned as shown in Figure 62.

The number of goals scored out of 20 attempts (taken from anywhere in the region of the shuttle) should be recorded. Following this the players take full rest. Repeat four times.

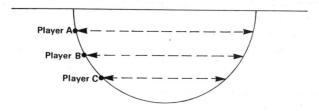

Player A : 10 shuttles ; Player B : 15 shuttles ; Player C : 20 shuttles
                    20 shots   20 shots   20 shots

Fig. 62

Task Two

Players start at goal post and complete task through to path 5 (see Fig. 63).

Players must take 30 second recovery before moving onto path 2 and repeating task; and so on through to path 5. A record of number of goals scored must be kept. Repeat four times, but full recovery is necessary before so doing.

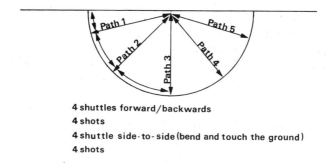

4 shuttles forward/backwards
4 shots
4 shuttle side-to-side (bend and touch the ground)

Fig. 63   4 shots

Defences

Task One

Players start at path 1, at the post, and shuttle forward and backwards (in the most efficient and appropriate way) 4 times (see Fig. 64). As the player reaches the post she must leap as if to intercept a high pass. *Using the goal*

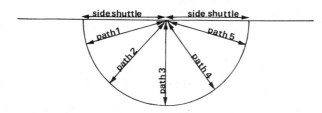

Fig. 64

line, the player does 4 side-to-side shuttles—bends and touches the floor. After a 60 seconds rest, they move to path 2 and repeat. At the end of path 5, players may rest but for no more than 5 minutes. Task is repeated 4 times in all.

Task Two
Two players are positioned as shown in Figure 65.

Player A feeds Player B with continuous high balls for 3 minutes. Players then change over, or take 3 minutes rest. Task is repeated twice.

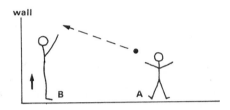

Fig. 65

Centre court

Task One
Task area is marked as shown in Figure 66.

Players complete the following:
1 Jump from 3' mark, as if to 'intercept', land and sprint to 10' mark—touch mark.
2 Sprint to 3' mark, jump to 'intercept', land and sprint to 20' mark—touch mark.
3 Sprint to 3' mark, jump to 'intercept,' land and sprint to 30' mark—touch mark.
4 Sprint to 3' mark, jump to 'intercept', land and spring to 20' mark—touch mark.
5 Continue through to 10' and, finally, 3' mark.
Players must rest for 1½ minutes before repeating—4 times.

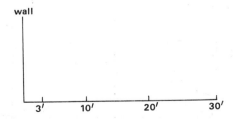

Fig. 66

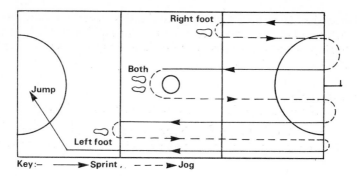

Fig. 67   Key:— ——▶ Sprint , — — —▶ Jog

Task Two

Figure 67 illustrates this task:

Players complete the following:

1 Sprint from goal-line to first third-line, jump and land on *right* foot, pivot quickly around on *left* foot, and jog back to goal-line.

2 Turn and sprint to centre circle, jump and land on *both* feet, pivot to the left, and jog back to goal-line.

3 Turn, sprint to second third-line, spring and land on *left* foot, pivot on *right* foot (to the right) and jog back to goal-line.

4 Turn and sprint the full court and jump to touch the goal net.

Players must rest for 1½ minutes before repeating, after which they must take a five minute rest before following on with task three.

Task Three

Figure 68 illustrates the task, which is followed on from task two with a five minute break in between.

Players complete as task two, with following exceptions:

1 Repeat 5 times through without rest.

2 Resting no longer than 3 minutes.

3 Repeat above 5 times.

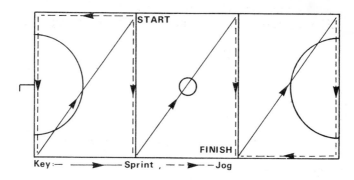

Fig. 68   Key :— ——▶ Sprint , — —▶ Jog

Coaching points
The above tasks are to stress (1) the speed with which players can change direction and (2) acceleration line with that change.

·CONCLUSION

There are many different ingredients in a good fitness programme, and they are all essential if players are to perform to maximum ability. There are no short cuts, and no easy way, to achieve top class condition. However, that does not mean that a dull and arduous schedule must be followed. With careful planning, fitness training can be varied and enjoyable.

Activities should be carefully selected; always bearing in mind the player's individual differences and needs. All players will benefit from some form of training—fitness must never be neglected.

Ten Basic Rules

The following ten basic rules will help in obtaining a fuller understanding of the game of netball. For further guidance and indepth knowledge of the rules it is advised that the reader consult the current rules book obtaining from the A.E.N.A.

RULE 1

The court is divided into five areas and a player, with or without the ball, is off-side if she enters any area other than her own playing area.

Playing areas for each player are as follows:

Court showing playing areas

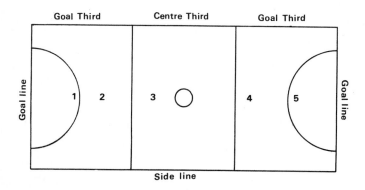

Permitted areas:

Goal Shooter : Area 1 and 2.
Goal Attack   : Area 1, 2 and 3.
Wing Attack   : Area 2 and 3.
Centre   : Area 2, 3 and 4.
Wing Defence : Area 3 and 4.
Goal Defence : Area 3, 4 and 5.
Goal Keeper   : Area 4 and 5.

Positions of players may only be changed during an interval, or after stoppage caused by illness or injury.

RULE 2

The game is controlled by two umpires, each being responsible for decisions in one half of the court. For this purpose the length of the court is divided in half across the centre from side to side-line.

The decision of the umpire is final and is given without appeal. She umpires according to the rules and decides on any matter not covered by the rules. The umpire should not penalise an infringement when by so doing she places the non offending team at a disadvantage. The umpire should not criticise or coach any team while a competition match is in progress.

RULE 3

There is a 3 second limit on a pass, throw-in, shot at goal, penalty pass or shot and free pass.

RULE 4

A penalty pass is awarded for the rules of *Contact, Obstruction* and *Intimidation.* When contact, obstruction and intimidation occurs inside the goal circle, either Goal Shooter or Goal Attack may take the penalty and may make a pass or shot for goal. A penalty may be defended by any opposing player allowed in the area, other than the offending player who shall stand beside and away from the thrower, taking no part in the play until the ball has left the thrower's hands.

RULE 5

The game is started and restarted after a goal, or after an interval by a centre pass taken alternately by the Centre of the opposing team. The centre pass must be caught or touched by a player allowed in the centre third.

RULE 6

Only the Goal Shooter or Goal Attack can score a goal. For a shot to be attempted the ball must be wholly caught inside the goal circle. A shot may be intercepted by the Goal Keeper or Goal Defence provided she maintains a distance of 3 feet measured on the ground between her nearer foot and the landing or pivoting foot of the shooter.

RULE 7

A player is in possession of the ball when she has control of it with one or both hands. A player may pass the ball in any manner except by rolling it.

The ball must be caught or touched in each third of the court. The ball cannot be hurled from one end of the court to the other. A player who is sitting, lying or kneeling on the ground cannot play the ball or attempt to gain possession of it.

RULE 8

A player may take one step after catching the ball. She may not reground her first landing foot until she has passed or shot.

RULE 9

A free pass is awarded for infringements on court other than those involving contact, obstruction, intimidation or simultaneous offences by two opposing players.

A throw-up is given between two opposing players who catch the ball simultaneously, catch the ball, send it out of the court, contact each other whilst striving to play the ball, or go off-side.

When the ball goes out of court, it is thrown-in by a player allowed in that particular area.

RULE 10

The game is of four quarters of 15 minute session, with an interval of 3 minutes between the first/second and third/fourth quarters, and with a maximum of 10 minutes at half-time. Teams change ends at each quarter.

When a player is ill or hurt, a stop of up to 5 minutes is allowed to decide whether the injured or sick player is fit to continue play. This decision is left to the teams' officials. Time lost for an accident, or any other cause, is added to that quarter of the game. Extra time is only allowed when a penalty pass or shot is taken.

Due to other circumstances (e.g. shortage of time in a triangular fixture), the game may be of two halves of 20 minutes each. The game may even be of a shorter duration in a tournament.

Appendix

USEFUL INFORMATION

The Governing Body of the sport

The All England Netball Association, Francis House, Francis Street, London SW1. (Telephone: 01-828 2176.)

AENA Publications and publicity aids

The following is available from the above address:
Official Netball Rules.
Netball Skills.
Junior Netball.
Pick-a-Practice Cards.
Official Score Sheet Pads.
Netball—The Official AENA Magazine.
Specimen Umpires' Written Test Papers.

Films

Aiming for Wembley. Apply to the All England Netball Association, Francis House, Francis Street, London, SW1. (Telephone: 01-828 2176.)

The World Championship—New Zealand 1975. Hire: Town and Country Productions Limited, 21 Cheyne Row, London SW3 5HP. *Booking Fee:* £4.75

Awards of the Governing Body

The Coaching and Umpiring Awards open to ordinary and associate members of the Association are in three grades:
Level 1   Regional Award
Level 2   Intermediate Award
Level 3   Panel Award
Umpiring has a further grade of International Award, which is open to panel umpires who are eligible to umpire at international matches.

Netball shooting badge scheme

Three levels of award are awarded:
3rd Class (Green badge)
2nd Class (Blue badge)
1st Class (Red badge)
For details of all the above awards contact the AENA at above address.

Netball posters
These posters illustrate the skills and tactics of the game, and are available from: Sports Posters, 9 Holt Road, Sheringham, Norfolk. (Telephone: 0263-823004.)

Popmobility

A useful training aid for flexibility and endurance. For details of LPs, tapes and demonstrations contact: Mr. Ken Woolcott, 24 Pasture Avenue, Wembley, Middlesex. (Telephone: 01-904 1745.)